The Toronto Underground Restaurant Book

CYNTHIA WINE

THE TORONTO
UNDERGROUND RESTAURANT BOOK

A Guide to Neighborhood Restaurants in Toronto

1986
Doubleday Canada Limited, Toronto, Canada
Doubleday and Company Inc., Garden City, New York

Canadian Cataloguing in Publication Data

Wine, Cynthia.
  The Toronto underground restaurant book

I S B N 0-385-25035-5
1. Restaurants, lunch rooms, etc. – Ontario – Toronto – Directories. I. Title.
TX910.C2W56 1986   647'.95713541   C86-093430-6

Library of Congress Cataloguing-in-Publication Data

Wine, Cynthia.
  The Toronto underground restaurant book

Includes index.
1. Restaurants, lunch rooms, etc. – Ontario – Toronto – Directories. I. Title.
TX910.C2W543 1986   647'.95713'541   86-4505
I S B N 0-385-25035-5

Design by The Dragon's Eye Press
Typesetting by Alphatext
Printed and bound in Canada by Gagne Printing

ACKNOWLEDGEMENTS

My gratitude is due to many people who lent advice and appetite to this project. They are: Don Kugler, Leah Cherniak, Ford Clements, Nancy and Stanley Colbert, Winston Collins, Marjorie Harris, Sheila Kieran, Charles Oberdorf, Mag Ruffman, Gail Singer, and Darryl Simmons.

For Shash and Carole

TABLE OF CONTENTS

INDEX

AFTER HOURS Restaurants open after 1 am.

After All
535 Mount Pleasant Rd.

Bar Diplomatico
594 College St.

Burger on Tap (weekends only)
2360 Yonge St.

By the Way Cafe
400 Bloor St. West

Commisso Bros.
8 Kincort St.

Dooney's Cafe
511 Bloor St. West

Fatso's (weekends only)
536 St. Clair Ave. West

Greek Islands Restaurant
888 Bloor St. West

Hunan Palace
421 Spadina Ave.

Jonathan's Hamburgers
1961 Queen St. East

Kam Kuk Yuen
472 Dundas St. W.

Living Well Cafe
692 Yonge St.

Massimo Pizza and Pasta
302 College St.

Odyssey (weekends only)
477 Danforth Ave.

Omonia (weekends only)
426 Danforth Ave.

People's Foods
176 Dupont St.

San Francesco (weekends only)
10 Clinton St.

Stella's (weekends only)
739 Queen St. East

Vesta Lunch
474 Dupont St.

Vesuvio's (weekends only)
3014 Dundas St. West

Wok and Bowl (weekends only)
195 Dundas St. West

PREFACE

A dozen years ago it was easy — you went to Fran's for rice pudding or to Murray's for eggs. Now there are so many small neighbourhood restaurants in Toronto that you could eat each meal in a different one for a year and still wonder what you're missing. The Yellow Pages directory alone lists 2,345 restaurants, and that doesn't take into account the specialty listings or the restaurants that have listings only in the white pages. And, there are all those spots that seem to have sprouted since the last time you meandered down a street. A thick book could be compiled about the places on Bloor Street alone.

The larger, more expensive restaurants are easier to decipher — they're regularly reviewed and usually they can afford to advertise. But the better beaneries are hard to find. Many of the small, ethnic, and individually owned places are promoted only by word of mouth and without some preview, may look intimidating. Restaurant food is one of the few commodities we buy without first examining it. You know what you're getting when you buy a sweater; you can feel it, turn it over, and try it on before you hand over your money. The only preview you have of most restaurant food is what you read on the menu. And by the time you see the actual food, it's yours.

This book has been assembled for people who love both good food and a bargain. All of the food described here has been touched and tasted.

The appetizing task of compiling a roster of these good but inexpensive restaurants was tackled initially with great enthusiasm. As the meals and months plodded on, however, the enthusiasm waned: where to start was easy; where to stop, impossible.

I have limited this collection to 180 places to eat, because I had to stop somewhere. This book does not pretend to be a definitive guide — if such a guide is even possible. It's a very personal guide, and if your favorite spot isn't in here, it doesn't mean that it's not great — I just haven't been there yet. Any suggestions would be welcomed for possible future revisions.

Many of the restaurants included here are known only to people within the neighborhoods where they're located. Information on some was relinquished reluctantly by those who frequent them. They fear that their favorite places cannot handle more people, and that if people outside the neighborhood learn about them, these places will become overcrowded and soon inaccessible to their longtime patrons. These same people also argue that operators of these small, one-of-a-kind restaurants would find it financially impossible to compete with the restaurant services provided by cost-efficient large chain operations.

I've discussed these possible dangers resulting from publicity with some owners of small restaurants, asking them if they wished to be subjected to demanding hordes of hungry people. "Subject me, please," they answer. "Anytime!"

In fact, some of Toronto's small restaurants operate on the edge of survival, and becoming better known could mean that they could continue to offer the same fine food at (one hopes) the same bargain prices.

The fact that many of the restaurants in this guide are individually run is often what's best about them. The resulting idiosyncrasies are fun: one eatery specializes in Hungarian food but carries South American newspapers because the owner's uncle drops in to read them, another gives free milk to members of a university football team, and another closes on January 6 (Ethiopian Christmas) because for them, it's a special holiday shared by no other restaurant in this listing.

These same idiosyncrasies can be inconvenient too. If papa decides that he wants to close at 10:35 P.M. on Friday this week because there's a family wedding on Saturday, close he does. If mama isn't there to make the special sauce for the hot veal sandwiches that day, you can have pizza instead or you can come another time.

xvi

Also, the mechanics of publication require that the manuscript must leave my hands several months before it reaches yours. Although a surprising number of the small places have been operating in exactly the same way for decades, some changes are common. For instance, price changes are brought about by changes in the minimum wage level and by inflation. There is no tax on meals priced under $1.00, but over $1.00 there's a 7% levy and there is a 10% tax on spirits and wines.

In this guide, we have provided as many specifics about hours, prices, methods of accepted payment and parking facilities as possible, but these also change for various reasons. Because of this we have included the telephone numbers for each restaurant (except for a couple that don't have phones). Please call ahead to confirm any information that is important to you. Or just go and take your chances — the number of terrific restaurants in Toronto these days is nothing short of phenomenal. I hope this collection will start you on your way.

Cynthia Wine
February, 1986

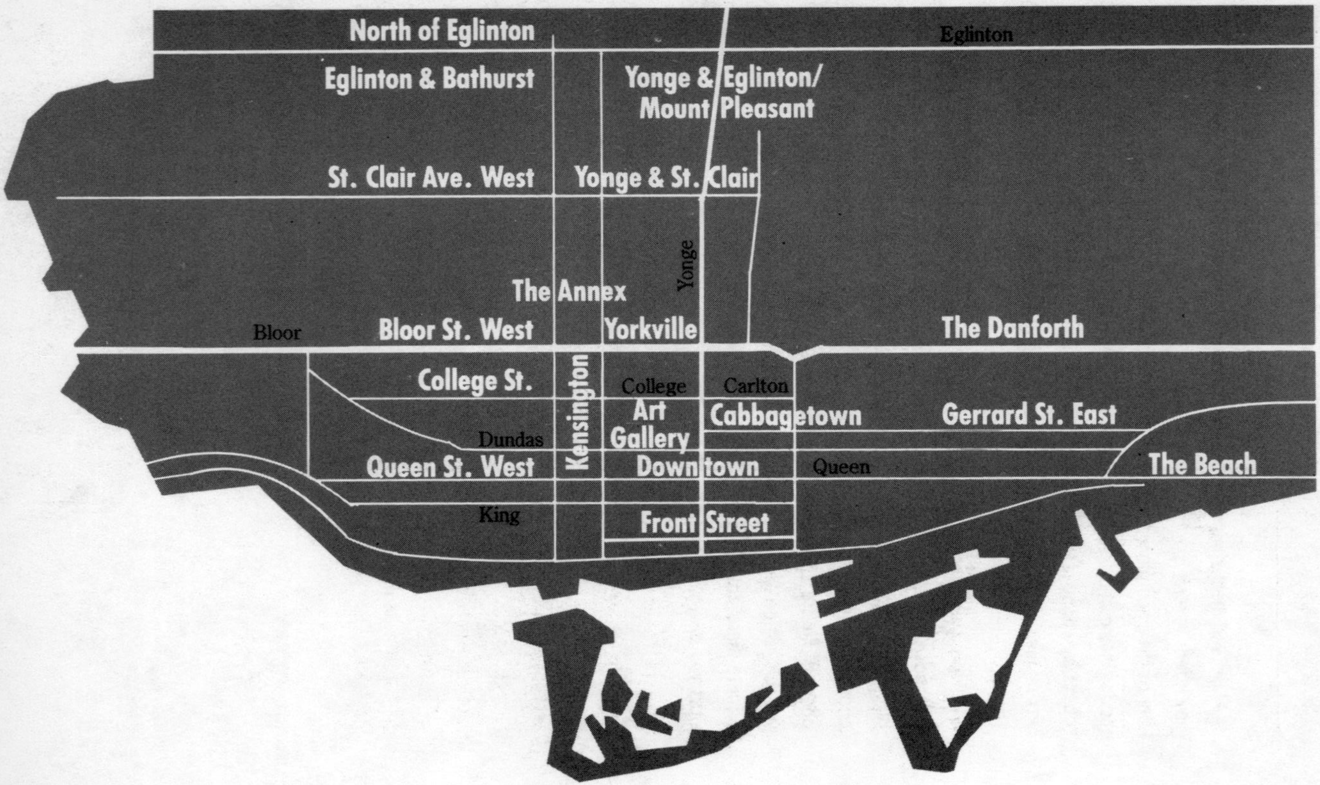
North of Eglinton
Eglinton
Eglinton & Bathurst
Yonge & Eglinton/
Mount Pleasant
St. Clair Ave. West
Yonge & St. Clair
Yonge
The Annex
Bloor
Bloor St. West
Yorkville
The Danforth
College St.
Kensington
College
Carlton
Art
Gallery
Cabbagetown
Gerrard St. East
Dundas
Queen St. West
Downtown
Queen
The Beach
King
Front Street

YORKVILLE AREA

Yorkville has had as many facelifts as the famous folk who are said to frequent its flashy watering holes. For the last two decades, the area has been a place where the curious come to watch others: in the sixties, the coffee shops featured two hippies to the twenty suburbanites who had come to see them or the motorcyclists who followed.

Eventually shock gave way to chic. For the last decade, this has been a ritzy area, and so is the food. There are a few exceptions — tucked-away places where you can find a pizza or a salad, or expensive restaurants that have an inexpensive gem on their menus. But there aren't many like the anachronistic Morrissey Tavern on Yonge Street, where you can get a grilled cheese sandwich for $1.00 in the seediest surroundings west of Jarvis Street. For those kind of low prices in Yorkville, watch for sidewalk vendors in the summer. In any season, try Dinah's Cupboard on Cumberland Street for a take-out sandwich or for fulsome butter tarts and Nanaimo bars.

The window seats at Bersani and Carlevale on Bloor and Bellair offer the best spot to watch the passing parade.

FIESTA RESTAURANT

You may have trouble spotting the Fiesta — some of the letters on the sign outside were missing when I was there. Inside, by peering through the darkness, you'll see a 1950s style of decor and dress. But the food — especially the soups and sandwiches — is always well tended. The clubhouse sandwich is very popular, but be prepared for odd extras, like apples, in this classic nosh ($5.55). The soups are hearty and wonderful. You can order a bowl with a half-sandwich which, considering the richness of the soups and the heartiness of the sandwiches, often is enough. Burgers are six ounces of juicy meat for $4.95, 75 cents extra for cheese or bacon. The Caesar salad is very good and very garlicky; large salad is $4.25 and still not big enough. Hot full meals are pricier, but the quality is reliable. Service can be grudging, and if you're there before they're prepared to serve dinner, you won't get any. Seating is in booths and on stools at a counter. There is a patio for the summer.

830 Yonge St. (near Cumberland St.)
924-1990
Hours: 11:30 A.M. to 1 A.M. Monday to
Saturday, 6 P.M. to 11 P.M. Sunday

Closed: All statutory holidays ("If the
banks are closed, we're closed.")
Licensed: Full
Payment: Visa, MasterCard
Parking: Municipal lot on
Cumberland St.

NOODLES BAR

The high tech bar with just stools for seating was added a few years ago to this chrome-and-orange Italian restaurant. The pasta is very good, as it is in the restaurant, but it's a little less pricey in the bar. Try too the fritto misto, a dish of deep fried calamari (squid), shrimp, and smelts ($5.50), or the spiffy pizza with ricotta cheese, crabmeat, olives, and fresh basil for $5.00.

60 Bloor St.
921-3171
Hours: Food is served in the bar from
    noon to 11 P.M. Monday to
    Saturday
Takeout available from attached area
    called the Bay Streetcar

Closed: Sunday; Christmas Day, Easter
Licensed: Full
Payment: Visa, MasterCard, AmEx
Parking: Nearby parking lots

I CARBONARI

I Carbonari took over just a couple of years ago from the Honeydew restaurant. Because of its odd location, only a few people found their way there originally. Once they did, they came back for the pizza, with its lovely thin crust and any number of combinations of Mediterranean flavors, including olive, artichoke, and tomato. The pizza is cooked in an open, wood fire in a brick oven ($6.50 for a ten-inch pizza with as many toppings as you wish). Also recommended is the insalata di arancie, a combination of oranges, garlic, and chilies (cayenne was used when I was there), tossed in olive oil and lemon. The pastas are good, if pricey.

102 Bloor St. W. (in back of building, facing Cumberland St. parking lot)
968-3572
Hours: Lunch: Noon to 3 P.M. Monday to Friday, Dinner: 6 P.M. to 10:30 P.M. Monday to Saturday

Closed: Sunday; statutory holidays
Licensed: Full
Payment: Visa, AmEx
Parking: Parking lot in front

GREG'S ICE CREAM & MIXIN'S

Greg's ice cream is so rich it's like cold, creamed custard. With so much cream and no preservatives, the ice cream melts on contact and must be eaten very quickly. That's no problem — the flavors are wonderful. Try the coconut, the rich and eggy vanilla, or any of the fruit ice creams. Watch for additional flavors like Oreo cookie, chocolate-banana, pears and ginger, and chocolate-orange (one scoop in a cone or cup is $1.30). Also, there are any number of mixings and toppings that may be added to the scoop, or buy a super-scoop and have your condiments mixed right in ($3.37). Mini-sundaes are two scoops, one topping, fresh whipped cream, and one condiment for $3.46. All of the ice cream is made on the premises. Greg's is very crowded on summer evenings.

200 Bloor St. W. (near Avenue Rd.)
961-4734
Hours: Summer: Noon to 11 P.M.
Sunday to Thursday, Noon to
midnight Friday, Saturday, Winter:
Noon to 10 P.M. Sunday to
Thursday, Noon to 11 P.M. Friday,
Saturday

Closed: Christmas Eve and Day, New
Year's Eve and Day
Licensed: No
Payment: Cash only

FIRESIDE LOUNGE,
WINDSOR ARMS HOTEL

At mid-afternoon, seven days a week, English tea is served at the Windsor Arms Hotel in a setting that's pretty and traditional enough even for the movie folk who pass by the door. This tea is not all liquid — it's an English cream tea, which means that a nice china potful of hot tea has a lot of food to keep it company. The food is served in four courses. First come dainty tea sandwiches of smoked salmon, cucumber, and watercress (of course). Next are the scones, with a bowlful of whipped cream (not Devon, sadly) and a caddy of fruit jelly. Butter the scones, pile on the cream, then top it with the jelly. Fruitcake comes next, then finally, a sweet that changes daily and may be raspberry mousse cake, or fruit flan. Your teacup is kept filled throughout. All this for $7.00 and you could call it dinner — food after this feast would be silly.

22 St. Thomas St. (south of
   Bloor St. W.)
979-2341
Hours: 3 P.M. to 6 P.M. seven days

Closed: Christmas Day
Licensed: Full (have some sherry)
Payment: Visa, MasterCard, AmEx
Parking: Underground at the Colonnade
   mall on Bloor St.

COPENHAGEN ROOM
(downstairs in the Danish Food Centre)

Upstairs there are open-faced sandwiches, salads, and hot soups, good and reasonably priced. Downstairs, items cost a bit more, but it's a wonderful place for lunch. A long, slender menu offers a terrific selection of open-faced sandwiches, and each is beautifully presented. Starburst at $7.95 is among the most expensive, but it contains fillets of plaice, shrimp, lumpfish caviar, and egg, with homemade mayonnaise. The gravlaks sandwich is the famous Scandinavian marinated salmon served with mustard and dill sauce ($5.95). Curried herring is an appetizer and sounds odd, but it is fabulous.

101 Bloor St. W. (at St. Thomas St.)
920-3287
Hours: 11:30 A.M. to 11:30 P.M.
   Monday to Saturday

Closed: Sunday; statutory holidays
Licensed: Full
Payment: Visa, MasterCard, AmEx
Parking: Underground at the Colonnade
   mall on Bloor St.

THE ANNEX

You may have trouble finding good food and good prices in other areas of Toronto, but not here. This is the area that services hungry students before they have expense accounts, and it is riddled with tiny eateries. Many of these are on the strip that runs along Bloor Street from Spadina Avenue to Bathurst Street. Some, like the Foodworks on Bloor west of Spadina, have great fries, others, like Jessie's a few doors east, offer very inexpensive sandwiches. The Serving Spoon has good pastries and cheeses. Further west, right at Bloor and Bathurst, Honest Ed's sells a good, cheap hot dog.

The Annex has maintained a few old diners that still serve rice pudding and clubhouse sandwiches. Be comforted: you will find nary a chicken wing nor a tomato rose at these places. Note the changes on Bathurst Street south of Dupont. In addition to the Jamaican fast-food shops and hamburger stops is an increasing number of small shops that sell homemade food and takeout sandwiches.

FALAFEL HUT

The most remarkable thing about the Falafel Hut is that, on Tuesdays, you can have a falafel for 99 cents. They cost $1.87 the rest of the time, but taste fine no matter what the price. Spinach pie, when it's fresh, is terrific, and so is the shawarma, a falafel-like sandwich with meat where the chick peas should be.

388 Bloor St. W. (near Walmer Rd.)
921-1674
– and –
2396 Bloor St. W. (near Jane St.)
769-9336
Hours: 10 A.M. to midnight Monday to
   Saturday, Noon to 10 P.M. Sunday

Closed: Christmas Day, New Years Day
Licensed: No
Payment: Visa
Parking: Parking lot on south side;
   some on street

BY THE WAY CAFÉ

It's odd to think of a place this offbeat as being "establishment", but in many ways By The Way set the tone for many of the other places along this strip. It began as a fried-chicken restaurant which, by the way, served the best yogurt in town. Later they subtracted the chicken, added the best hummus, the best babaganoush, and the best tabbouleh. And finally, chicken, in the form of very good wings found its way back. I'm partial to the Nanaimo bars and to any of the cream soups. The meals are snacky and very good. It could be called fast food, if the service wasn't so slow. The restaurant is sloppily casual, somewhat musty and, with its bearded clientele, there's a 1960s feel to the place. Summer evenings on the outdoor patio, a frozen yogurt in hand, are great fun.

400 Bloor St. W. (near Brunswick Ave.)
967-4295
Hours: Summer: 11 A.M. to 3 A.M. seven days, Winter: 11 A.M. to 3 A.M. Friday, Saturday, Sunday, 11 A.M. to 2 A.M. Monday to Thursday

Closed: Christmas Day, major Jewish holidays
Licensed: Yes
Payment: Visa
Parking: On street; municipal lot one block west

TAROGATO RESTAURANT

The popularity of each of the many schnitzel houses along Bloor Street West ebbs and grows, but the Tarogato seems to have maintained a loyal clientele that may drift, but eventually returns. Customers like the wiener schnitzel with bread and salad ($6.25), the cabbage rolls ($5.25), or the inexpensive goulash or bean soups ($1.80 and $1.60, respectively). The portions of the hearty Hungarian food are very generous and quite cheap. South American newspapers are available here because the uncle of one of the owners once lived in Argentina.

553 Bloor St. W. (near Bathurst St.)
536-7566
Hours: Noon to midnight Monday to
    Thursday, Noon to 1 A.M. Friday,
    Saturday, Noon to 11 P.M. Sunday

Closed: Christmas Day
Licensed: Wine and beer
Payment: Visa, MasterCard, AmEx
Parking: Street

BLUE CELLAR ROOM

 The Blue Cellar is part of the L'Europe Hungarian restaurant, but it is included in this guide because of its particularly cheap prices and generous quantities. With those amenities, it's no wonder that its most reliable customers are local students. They like the chicken paprikash, served with rice or potatoes and a vegetable, or the schnitzel with the same accompaniments ($4.50 for each). Milk is served free to members of the Varsity Blue teams.

469 Bloor St. W. (near Brunswick Ave.)
921-6269
Hours: Noon to 1 A.M. Monday to
    Saturday, Noon to 11 P.M. Sunday

Closed: Christmas Day, Boxing Day
Licensed: Full
Payment: Visa, MasterCard, AmEx,
    Diners Club
Parking: Street, side streets

CALANDRIA

Calandria is attached to the Harbord Bakery, which will give some clue as to the high quality of the food served here. The emphasis is Mediterranean: the spanakopita (spinach and cheese pie) is buttery, flaky, and superb; the tabbouleh is great, as is the Greek salad made with olives that have been marinated in wine. Empanadas are pastry turnovers filled with spicy chicken and vegetables. The stuffed grape leaves are good, and don't pass up the chopped liver. Everything is carefully made and seasoned. If the double-chocolate cookies are available, take out a mortgage and buy some. They are pricey, but in this case, money *can* buy happiness.

117 Harbord St. (Spadina Ave., south of Bloor)
929-5246
Hours: 10 A.M. to 6 P.M. Monday to Saturday

Closed: Sunday (but some things are available in the bakery, which is open); statutory and major Jewish holidays
Licensed: No
Payment: Visa
Parking: Street

BOULEVARD CAFÉ

The Boulevard is a pleasantly understated restaurant that specializes in Peruvian food. Some of the sandwiches and snacks can be quite inexpensive and a lot of fun. One of the most popular dinner dishes is the brochettes; they range in price depending on the type of meat or seafood chosen. The most popular is the chicken ($8.95), but try the sea bass, too. Mussels are cooked in wine and spices and served with linguine or spicy beans. Lamb is marinated, charcoal-broiled, and served in a Peruvian garlic sauce. Check the daily specials.

161 Harbord St. (near Borden St., west of Spadina Ave.)

961-7676

Hours: Lunch: Noon to 4 P.M. Monday to Saturday, Dinner: 5:30 P.M. to 10:30 P.M. Monday to Thursday, 5:30 P.M. to 11:30 P.M. Friday, Saturday, 5:30 P.M. to 10 P.M. Sunday, Brunch: 11 A.M. to 4 P.M. Sunday

Closed: Statutory holidays, the week between Christmas and New Year's

Licensed: Full

Payment: Visa, MasterCard, AmEx

Parking: Street

KORONA RESTAURANT

This is one of the nicer of the numerous schnitzel restaurants that cover the block from Spadina Avenue to Bathurst Street as generously as a schnitzel covers a plate. The Korona's decor is a bit better than some, and usually the food is, too; the prices are comparable.

A plateful of wiener schnitzel costs $5.25 including tax. The Wooden Platter, also standard fare, is enormous and comprises steak, liver, sausages, and onion rings, priced at $13 for two people. But you should be aware that this platter for two could serve a boarding house. The mixed grill includes wiener schnitzel, roast pork, cabbage rolls, potato, and beets. Veal paprikash costs $5.25 and has good, small dumplings. What's more, there are as many as twenty items that aren't listed on the menu.

Korona has live music, which doesn't help the digestion but at least is a diversion from all that chewing. The staff is very congenial. Owner George Malaya apologizes that they don't take credit cards, but claims it's because the staff all wear glasses and make too many mistakes with that funny plastic and all its odd numbers.

---

493 Bloor St. W. (near Brunswick Ave.)
961-1824
Hours: 10 A.M. to 11 P.M. "eight days a
  week"
Takeout also

Closed: Christmas Day, New Year's Day
Licensed: Full
Payment: Bring cash
Parking: Street; parking lot one block
  west.

CAFÉ MARIKO

Homey-nice food at very good prices is featured at this small, tidy Japanese restaurant. Where else can you get seven pieces of sushi for $6.95 ($7.95 at dinner)? Teriyaki (barbecued) chicken, beef, or tofu is $5.50 at lunch, $5.90 at dinner. The gyoza dumplings are wonderful: wonton wrappers filled with ground beef and vegetables, steamed and fried ($5.50 at lunch, $5.90 at dinner). Miso soup is $1.00. Don't look for a spoon – you drink it like tea.

298 Brunswick Ave. (south of
  Bloor St. W.)
968-0883
Hours: Lunch: Noon to 2:30 P.M.
  Tuesday to Friday, Dinner: 5 P.M. to
  9:30 P.M. Tuesday to Sunday

Closed: Monday; extended closing
  between Christmas and New Year's
Licensed: Beer and wine
Payment: Visa
Parking: Street

MADISON AVENUE RESTAURANT

This is the type of pub that everyone who has ever wanted to own a pub, wants to own. Chummy, warm, and beautiful, the three floors of this converted house are always full — even impassable at peak times. Some of the loyalists argue that the Madison Avenue has the best chicken wings in town. For $4.55, a pound of them is served Buffalo-style with celery, carrots, and blue cheese dressing. The wings are tart, as if they'd been marinated in lemon juice, then flavoured with honey garlic or spiced from mild to suicide. This suicide won't kill you. Hamburgers at $3.50 plus 50 cents a topping are juicy and generous in their little crusty bread rolls. Always watch for specials, like the steak-and-kidney pie ($5.25) or the rabbit stew ($5.50). From 3 P.M. to 7 P.M. on weekdays, tiger shrimp, mussels, and escargot are very cheap. There are over two dozen labels of beer, imported and domestic, to speed it all down.

14 Madison Ave. (east of Spadina Ave., north of Bloor St. W.)
927-1722
Hours: 11 A.M. to 1 A.M. Monday to Saturday, Noon to 11 P.M. Sunday

Closed: Never
Licensed: Yes
Payment: Visa, MasterCard, AmEx
Parking: Street

DOONEY'S CAFÉ

In the few years since it opened, Dooney's has become one of the most popular meeting places along this strip. The late week-night closing is a great boon. There are salads and light meals, but people come for the talk, the cappuccino, and the homemade ice creams. The cakes, including the bestselling chocolate mousse cake, are from Dufflet's.

511 Bloor St. W. (near Borden St.)
536-3293
Hours: 10 A.M. to 2 A.M. Monday to
    Saturday, 10 A.M. to 1 A.M. Sunday

Closed: Christmas Eve
Licensed: Full
Payment: Visa, MasterCard
Parking: Street; municipal lot at rear.

AVENUE COFFEE SHOP

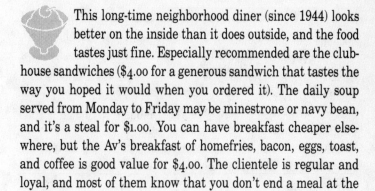 This long-time neighborhood diner (since 1944) looks better on the inside than it does outside, and the food tastes just fine. Especially recommended are the clubhouse sandwiches ($4.00 for a generous sandwich that tastes the way you hoped it would when you ordered it). The daily soup served from Monday to Friday may be minestrone or navy bean, and it's a steal for $1.00. You can have breakfast cheaper elsewhere, but the Av's breakfast of homefries, bacon, eggs, toast, and coffee is good value for $4.00. The clientele is regular and loyal, and most of them know that you don't end a meal at the Av without a serving of the exceptional rice pudding.

222 Davenport Rd. (near Avenue Rd.)
924-5191
Hours: 6 A.M. to 5 P.M. Monday to
    Friday, 6 A.M. to 3 P.M. Saturday

Closed: Sunday; statutory holidays
Licensed: No
Payment: Cash only
Parking: Some on street; nearby
    parking lots

THE FISH & CHIP SHOPPE

The three kinds of fish available here — halibut, cod and sole, are cut fresh every day from the whole fish. Each order includes 4 ounces of fish sealed into a crispy batter. Everything is homemade, including the chips, cole slaw and ice cream. Halibut with chips is $3.65; cod is $3.90 and sole is $3.30. Shrimps and assorted salads are also available.

There's a small eating area but takeout is more common. Doug Casimira has been operating the Fish & Chip Shoppe for 10 years and claims that the food is good because fish is their only business.

287 Davenport Rd.
964-0053
Hours: 11 A.M. to 8 P.M. Monday to
   Saturday
Takeout also

Closed: Sunday, statutory holidays
Licensed: No
Payment: Cash
Parking: Street, small lot beside
    building

CASTLE DRAGON

Castle Dragon is a neighborhood restaurant that people apologize for when they recommend it to their friends. Breakfasts are great, they'll say, but the place is a little ... umm ... casual. It's more than casual — it's downright tacky — but here's breakfast: two eggs, five strips of bacon, homefries, and toast for $1.75! Castle Dragon is really a Chinese restaurant, where they serve old-style Cantonese food (chow mein and the like) but breakfast is better.

292 Dupont St. (near Spadina Ave.)
968-9366
Hours: 7 A.M. to 11 P.M. Monday to
  Saturday

Closed: Sunday; statutory holidays
Licensed: Full
Payment: Cash only
Parking: Street

INDIAN RICE FACTORY

This is a long-loved local Indian restaurant with a loyal clientele that includes a tiny mouse with an asbestos palate. Particularly recommended are the Indian breads. Order them instead of rice. Chole is chickpeas with a tangy tomato sauce served with puri ($6.75). The chicken curry is cooked in ginger, garlic, and tomatoes, for $6.25. Another favorite dish is eggplant with sliced ginger, tomatoes, green pepper, and coriander. The thali dinner is served in the traditional divided metal plate. It's a great meal for the undecided, or for thali fans, for $9.95. Owner Amar Patel does all the cooking herself.

414 Dupont St. (near Howland Ave.)
961-3472
Hours: 11 A.M. to 11 P.M. seven days

Closed: Never
Licensed: Full
Payment: Visa, MasterCard, AmEx,
　　　　　Diners Club
Parking: Street

VESTA LUNCH

Vesta is a sinister-looking lunch counter at the corner of Bathurst and Dupont streets that is recommended only for the brave or for those who are in love with its clubhouse sandwiches ($3.75). The service is gruff, the atmosphere is awful, and you can have it all at any hour of the day or night any day of the year. Vesta never, never closes. It can't – the locks on the door are never used.

474 Dupont St. (at Bathurst St.)
537-4318
Hours: 24 hours, seven days

Closed: Never
Licensed: No
Payment: Cash only
Parking: Street

PEOPLE'S FOODS

Everyone in the area knows People's, because for sixteen years they've been able to stop there at any hour and fill up. All-day breakfast, including homefries and toast with the bacon and eggs, is $3.20 including tax. The sandwiches, especially the chicken and egg salad, are fulsome; the clubhouse sandwich is made with breast of chicken and, for $4.95, tastes like clubhouse sandwiches should. Hamburgers are charcoal broiled and served with cole slaw. Please leave room for the rice pudding. Next to that at the Mars Restaurant on College Street, People's rice pudding is the best in the city. People's is a small, very casual restaurant with eight tables and a few stools.

176 Dupont St. (near St. George St.)
961-3171
Hours: 24 hours, seven days

Closed: Christmas Day, New Year's Day
Licensed: No
Payment: Cash only
Parking: Street; parking lot next door

ANNAPURNA VEGETARIAN RESTAURANT

Annapurna has been serving some of the best vegetarian food in Toronto for more than a dozen years. Prices are low, quality and portion-size are high. It is a pleasant restaurant with fourteen tables and a firm no-smoking rule.

The Indian assortment costs $10 for two people and includes samosa, bhajia (vegetable fritter), potato masala, spinach curry, puri, and papadum. The Indian specials are not served between 3 P.M. and 5 P.M., but are available during lunch and dinner hours. A dish of mushrooms and zucchini in a yogurt sauce is served with honey-ginger carrots and rice croquettes for $4.00. Spinach lasagna is the same price. Watch for the international buffet held from 3 P.M. to 5 P.M. on occasional Sundays, a day they're normally closed.

1085 Bathurst St. (south of Dupont St.)
537-8513
Hours: Noon to 9 P.M. Monday to
  Saturday

Closed: Sunday; last two weeks of
  April and August (for religious
  retreats)
Licensed: No
Payment: Cash only
Parking: Street

ART GALLERY AREA

Sandwiched between Kensington Market and Chinatown and underpinned by Queen Street West, the Art Gallery of Ontario is surrounded by some of the best snacking places in Toronto. A stroll along Baldwin Street east of McCaul Street will reveal a new spot each time this route is taken. The Village by the Grange, across the street from the gallery, is a cornucopia of eateries. The mall inside has a "gourmet corner" like shopping plazas everywhere, but this one is different: each stand is individually operated, often by families. The same hearty ethnic sandwiches can be found here as on an odyssey along Bloor Street — but it's warm inside the Village by the Grange.

The Young Lok Chinese restaurant, long loved for its palace shrimp and other Cantonese specialities, now also has a location in the Village by the Grange.

YUNG SING PASTRY SHOP

Well known in the neighborhood, this small shop has provided many a lunch for local students and for those with any appetite left over after a long shop at the nearby Kensington Market. Sweet-savory yeast buns are filled with spicy meats or vegetables: beef, chicken, curried beef, ham and egg, pork, vegetables alone, or coconut, for only 75 cents each — but one is never enough. Yung Sing also offers hot-and-sour soup ($1.35), vegetarian Singapore rice ($1.95), and a selection of Chinese pastries. This has been a popular spot for over ten years. There is only one small table, so be prepared for takeout. In summer, there are places to sit outside.

22 Baldwin St. (near McCaul St.)
979-2832
Hours: 11 A.M. to 6 P.M. seven days
Takeout mainly

Closed: Never
Licensed: No
Payment: Cash only
Parking: Street

GYPSY HUNGARIAN
RESTAURANT

One might think that a large flap of schnitzel was fodder enough, but here that hearty delicacy is taken a few steps further. It is encased in two large pieces of rye, and some mustard, mayonnaise, and maybe some peppers are added to make Gypsy's schnitzel sandwich. You can have just the sandwich for $3.27 including tax (and heaven knows that would be enough), or you can have a dinner of it, which includes salad and fries, for $4.95 including tax. Gypsy's also has cabbage rolls and soups. It is one of the food outlets inside the Village by the Grange, and there are tables in the mall where you can eat and watch the people go by.

105 McCaul St. (in the Village by the
    Grange)
598-1650
Hours: 10 A.M. to 8 P.M. Monday to
    Friday, 11 A.M. to 6 P.M. Saturday,
    Sunday
Takeout only (tables in the mall)

Closed: Easter, Good Friday, Christmas
    Day, Boxing Day, New Year's Day
Licensed: No
Payment: Cash only
Parking: Some on street; underground
    parking lot

HOUSE OF NOODLES INC.

The success of this small, dim restaurant prompted the owners to open the brighter and bigger one at the corner of Spadina Avenue and Dundas Street West. The new restaurant is fine if you order noodles. However, prices are cheaper and the food is better at the first location, restoring faith in that old cliché about Chinese restaurants — the more lowly the spot, the better the food. The firm, eggy noodles for both restaurants are made in the basement on Grange Avenue. Most of them are sold to other restaurants, but some are saved for the folks upstairs. The noodles are offered in a rich chicken broth, to which is added any of a catalogue of savory fixings. The additions determine the price, so shrimp noodles will cost more than chicken and less than lobster, but it's hard to spend much more than $6.00 for dinner here.

54 Grange Ave. (near Beverley St.)
596-8636
Hours: 11 A.M. to midnight, seven days

Closed: Never
Licensed: No
Payment: Visa
Parking: Parking lot nearby

UKRAINIAN PEROGY HUT

Start with the borscht for 95 cents, and proceed to the perogies (eight for $2.65), using sour cream to embellish both the soup and the dumplings. Try the cabbage rolls, also (three of them are $2.85).

(Village by the Grange mall)
598-4916
Hours: 8 A.M. to 8 P.M. Monday to
    Friday, 8 A.M. to 6 P.M. Saturday, 9
    A.M. to 5 P.M. Sunday
Takeout only (tables in the mall)

Closed: Statutory holidays
Licensed: No
Payment: Cash
Parking: Underground

ELENA'S

Surely the biggest souvlaki in town is served here — in a pita or in a sub-bun, this sloppy wonderful mess of meat, vegetables, and tzadziki takes a long time to eat. It probably should be eaten in a bathtub. But be undaunted: the owners offer written eating instructions. They suggest you unwrap the sandwich as you would peel a banana, just enough to allow a big bite from the top as you hold the bottom tight. Price depends on the meat you order: pork is $3.50 and beef is $3.95. The same meat (but more of it) on a plate with Greek salad and a dinner roll costs $4.75 for pork, and $5.75 for beef. Elena's has soup for starters and baklava for a finish, but it is unlikely you'll be able to cope with either with the huge main course.

71 McCaul (Village by the Grange mall)

977-7362

Hours: 11:30 A.M. to 8 P.M. Monday to Friday, 12 noon to 6 P.M. Saturday

Takeout only (tables in mall)

Closed: Sunday; statutory holidays

Licensed: No

Payment: Cash only

Parking: Underground

SATE

Sate, pronounced "satay," is strips of marinated meat strung on a bamboo skewer, grilled and served with a spicy peanut sauce. It is sold by street vendors throughout Indonesia. At this stand in Village by the Grange, you can get very good sate for 80 cents a skewer. This stand also has Korean origins so, for a side order, you can have kim chee, which is very, very, hot, pickled cabbage for $1.00 — an addictive salad, especially if you're inclined toward eating fire.

(Village by the Grange mall)
596-0339
Hours: 10 A.M. to 8 P.M. Monday to
    Saturday
Takeout only (tables in mall)

Closed: Sunday; statutory holidays
Licensed: No
Payment: MasterCard
Parking: Underground

EATING COUNTER

This is a favorite local restaurant with a slightly different flavor than the other Chinese restaurants a few blocks south on Dundas Street West. Try the beef with satay sauce (a spicy dish with lots of vegetables, $5.50), the shrimp with lemon ($7.25), and especially the deep-fried squid ($5.50). Food is relatively inexpensive and reliable in this casual eatery. Its popularity prompted the opening of Eating Counter II on Danforth Avenue.

41 Baldwin St. (near Beverley St.)
977-7028
Hours: 11 A.M. to 11 P.M. seven days

Closed: Never
Licensed: No
Payment: Cash only
Parking: Street

ARC COURT DIM SUM RESTAURANT

Arc Court is a pleasant, bright restaurant with less than a dozen tables, which usually are full. It is best known for the dim sum, which are served all day. There is no trolley here: each dim sum is steamed to order. That and the freshness of ingredients makes Arc Court's dim sum special. A dim sum lunch for two will cost about $10; for dinner, approximately $15.

15 St. Andrew St.
598-1823
Hours: 8 A.M. to midnight seven days

Closed: Chinese New Year
Licensed: Full
Payment: Visa
Parking: Parking lot across the street
will refund first hour of parking on
orders of $10 and more

KENSINGTON
MARKET/SPADINA

The flavors of the Kensington Market and Spadina Avenue south of College Street have varied over the years, depending on which immigrant group predominated there. The market was almost exclusively Jewish until the late 1950s; now it is predominantly Portuguese, with some West and East Indian merchants and some middle-European and Chinese.

Spadina Avenue now has a great many Chinese restaurants, but you can still stop by Switzer's Delicatessen for a knish or a hot corned beef sandwich. Both on Spadina Avenue and in the market, watch for juicy sausages on kaisers and little places that serve dim sum.

Susan Oppenheim, a Toronto singer, operates a lovely little bed-and-breakfast home in the area. Call her ahead of time at 598-4562 and go for breakfast before you start your day. You can have French toast, fruit plate, fish (on Sundays only), or almost anything for about $7.00 for a full meal.

THE BAGEL

The Bagel is among the longest-loved Jewish eateries in town. That it remains popular is attested to by its noisy crowding at prime times, and by the photos that loyal celebrities have sent to be affixed to the restaurant's walls. Customers are far from coddled here, but they are fed some wonderful fare: borscht, winter or summer, is super; chopped liver, sweet and sour meatballs, gefilte fish — they're all great. My favorite among the egg dishes is the eggs, lox, and onions, because the onions are fried dark and sweet and they are plentiful. Bagel sandwiches are generous and good, but don't ask them to toast your bagel because they won't do it — ever. Prices for egg dishes range from $1.90 to $5.30; the sandwiches from $1.80 to $3.85.

285 College St. (near Spadina Ave.)
923-0171
Hours: 7 A.M. to 10 P.M. seven days

Closed: Major Jewish holidays
Licensed: No
Payment: Cash only
Parking: Street

UNITED BAKERS
DAIRY RESTAURANT

You may already have discovered that the best Jewish foods aren't necessarily the main-course dishes, especially if these are made of meat. Koshered and kilned roasts are, to put it charitably, a bit dry. What's really good are the foods that go before and after main courses — the little nosh. Often the best of them are not in the meat category at all, but are dairy foods. United Bakers has fabulous Jewish dairy food. The soups, especially the barley, split pea (with noodles), or the borschts ($1.85), are the best in the city — no, make that the world. Cheese blintzes are large, round crepes filled with sweetened cheese and served with applesauce and sour cream ($5.75). Gefilte fish (a large fish dumpling — but to call United's gefilte fish a dumpling is like calling caviar "fish eggs") is served with beet-reddened horseradish, hot enough to make you remember it for a long while. The menu is very large and very good. The restaurant is casual, with its arborite counters and friendly service. A bigger and brighter version opened a couple of years ago at Bathurst Street and Lawrence Avenue West, but this is where it all started. United Bakers has been a family-run operation since 1912.

338 Spadina Ave. (north of Dundas St. W.)
593-0697
Hours: 6 A.M. to 7 P.M. Monday to Thursday, 6 A.M. to 4 P.M. Friday, 8 A.M. to 4 P.M. Summer Sundays

Closed: Saturday, Sunday in winter
Licensed: No
Payment: Cash only
Parking: Street; parking lot to the north

LEE GARDEN

Look behind the door when you enter and you'll see stickers attached to the window that proclaim Lee Garden to be a good place. Lee Garden was discovered, without the help of guide books, by the Chinese food aficionados who continue to fill the large room. There are a few private tables, but mostly there are large, round, communal ones, covered with plastic, where people are seated in order of arrival.

The fish and shellfish dishes are particularly recommended. These will vary with availability, so check with the waiter. If it's available, the baked shrimp with pepper is very good ($6.75). Lee Garden is known also for its Mongolian hot pot, a huge, hearty meal for two or more of meat, seafood, and vegetables, cooked at the table ($16.95). The hot pot is available only in the winter; start asking for it after mid-October. Note that the restaurant closes earlier than many of the Chinese restaurants in the area.

358 Spadina Ave. (south of College St.)
593-9524
Hours: 4 P.M. to 11:30 P.M. Tuesday to
   Sunday

Closed: Monday
Licensed: No
Payment: Visa
Parking: Street; parking lot at back

HUNAN PALACE

The Hunan has survived the vicissitudes of fashion — in Chinese cookery and in fickle audiences — and although now its biggest fans seem to come from the suburbs, the food is very good. This is a restaurant with a mammoth menu, where it pays to watch what's traveling to the other tables before you order. Szechuan clichés like orange beef with chilies is very good here. So are the dumplings, the spicy green beans and fish, and shellfish dishes.

412 Spadina Ave. (near Huron St.)
593-9381
Hours: 9 A.M. to 4 A.M. seven days

Closed: Never
Licensed: Beer and wine
Payment: Visa, MasterCard, AmEx
Parking: Street

THE GREAT WALL RESTAURANT

This is a restaurant of long standing and good reputation among the hundreds of pretty good Chinese
restaurants in the area. It's large, with a more subdu-
ed air than its popularity would suggest. When the Szechuan,
Hunan, and Peking food is good here, it's really good.

Hot and sour soup is both, as well as being thick, rich, and flavorful. Green beans, Szechuan-style ($5.75), are popular in the
local Szechuan restaurants and here they're as good as they get.
Try the eggplant, which is fried in peanut oil and chilies, with
pureed peanuts. Try the dumplings too.

There are, in fact, dozens of dishes to try. The best guide is not
the gargantuan menu, which reads like a telephone book, but
the evening's specials penned in black marker and attached to
the folding screens. That list is shorter and has dishes that are
easier to understand, or at least easier to ask the helpful wait-
ers about. If there's fresh seafood (especially clams, mussels, or
squid, in any kind of spicy sauce), order it because it's always
wonderful.

To its credit, the restaurant always tries to have the freshest
of vegetables in season. Menu items are written in English,
which is helpful since most of the clientele is Caucasian. Imported beer is available, which goes well with Chinese food.

---

444 Spadina Ave. (just south of College St.)

961-5554

Hours: Noon to 10 P.M. Monday to Thursday, Noon to 11 P.M. Friday, Saturday, 1 P.M. to 10 P.M. Sunday

Closed: Almost never

Licensed: Full

Payment: Visa, MasterCard, AmEx

Parking: Street

CREST GRILL

The stack of small iron frying pans gives you the best clue as to why you're here: the Crest makes wonderful eggs — fried, scrambled, however you want them. They are so well made that a spiffy uptown restaurant got the Crest's cook to show them how. Full breakfast is $2.30 to $2.95. Freshly squeezed orange juice is 70 cents or $1.40. The area is a bit seamy and the place sort of suspicious looking, so people don't often go there unless they are sent. Consider yourself sent.

446½ Spadina Ave. (just north of
   College St.)
922-4715
Hours: 7 A.M. to 8 P.M. seven days

Closed: Never
Licensed: No
Payment: Cash only
Parking: Street

SPADINA GARDEN

 The specialties are Kiangsi, Szechuan, and Hunan, which means hot and aromatic. One of the advantages to this flavorful food is that MSG is not necessary.

Recommended dishes include orange beef, general chicken (hot peppers, aromatic oils, green pepper, and onion), garlic shrimp made with tree fungus or cloud-ear mushrooms, garlic, and those aromatic oils. The house special noodle dish is $4.95. Be sure to try the dumplings — they're super, juicy, and full.

Spadina Garden shares the block with the Hunan Palace and Chong Star House, each of which has the essentially the same menu. These restaurants all change in quality month by month, depending on their chefs and their popularity.

---

461 Spadina Ave. (near College St.)
598-2734
Hours: Noon to 11 P.M. seven days

Closed: Never
Licensed: Full
Payment: Visa, MasterCard, AmEx
Parking: Street

KAM KUK YUEN RESTAURANT

The most popular dishes here are the barbecued pork and duck. Suckling pig is also offered. All are available for eating in or for takeout. On takeout, pork is $4.60 a pound, half a duck is $7.50, and suckling pig is $8.50 a pound. Whether you take your order out or eat at one of the restaurant's sixteen tables, you'll also be tempted by the Cantonese fried noodle (pork, beef, and vegetables, stir fried and laid on top of crispy brown noodles) or the spicy soya sauce chicken.

472 Dundas St. W. (near Spadina Ave.)
977-0433
Hours: 10 A.M. to 2 A.M. seven days
Takeout also

Closed: Never
Licensed: Full
Payment: Visa, MasterCard
Parking: Street; parking lot one block south

REBELO'S KENSINGTON SUPERMARKET

The family business was just down the street for 20 years, and has been in this new location for about a year. Rebelo's is a supermarket only, but they do a great business in takeout cooked fish. Try the barbecued sardines, sole in egg, and baked tuna. Fish is sold by the pound ranging from $3.69 to $5.00.

60 Kensington Ave.
593-2784
Hours: 8 A.M. to 8 P.M. Monday,
    Saturday, 8 A.M. to 9 P.M. Thursday,
    Friday
Takeout only

Closed: Sunday, Tuesday, Wednesday;
    all statutory holidays
Licensed: No
Payment: Cash only
Parking: Street; municipal lot (they'll
    pay for the first hour if your order is
    more than $20.)

KENSINGTON PATTY PALACE

So far, this is the home of the best West Indian patties in the neighborhood — they're big, juicy, and fearlessly spicy (beef or vegetable, 65 cents). Roti ranges in price from $1.25 to $3.50, depending on whether you have it plain or with beef, goat, chicken, or chickpea. Soup of the day may be red pea, goat, beef, or chicken (80 cents or $1.20). Either eat there standing up, or take it out.

172 Baldwin St. (near Kensington Ave.)
596-6667
Hours: 9 A.M. to 6 P.M. Monday to
    Wednesday, Saturday, 9 A.M. to 7
    P.M. Thursday, 9 A.M. to 8 P.M.
    Friday
Takeout mainly

Closed: Sunday; statutory holidays
Licensed: No
Payment: Cash only
Parking: Some on street

EUROPEAN QUALITY MEATS & SAUSAGES

This is a wonderful, bustling meat market, well known for its good prices and European cuts of meat. It's less known for its ready-to-eat snack — one of its own hearty, spicy, homemade sausages, served hot on a sesame-egg bun (sauerkraut optional) for only 99 cents. There is no seating.

176 Baldwin St. (in Kensington Market)
596-8691
Hours: 8 A.M. to 7 P.M. Monday to
    Wednesday, 8 A.M. to 8 P.M.
    Thursday, 7:30 A.M. to 9 P.M. Friday,
    7:30 A.M. to 7 P.M. Saturday
Takeout only

Closed: Sunday
Licensed: No
Payment: Cash only
Parking: Parking lot to the east

QUEEN STREET WEST

The stretch of shops and restaurants on Queen Street between University and Spadina avenues has changed completely in feeling in the last five years. Once run-down, it is now very trendy. The food is casual, but offered with the same avant-garde humor of the clothing and accessories shops.

Many of the restaurants serve food based on a natural philosophy, and nearly all feature wide vegetarian selections. The Parrot is a wonderful place for brunch, and the French cafés are fine for dinners. But don't get lost in the newness and miss legendary Barney's (see the review).

In the summers, look for Gordon's Cart, usually parked in the shade. He makes wonderful sandwiches and chapatis. Continuing west, watch for the profusion of shops blossoming around Bathurst Street, and for the occasional culinary gems that may be gleaned in Parkdale.

QUEEN MOTHER CAFÉ

This could be described as a theme restaurant, with the theme being post-war, the early 1950s. Despite the number of people constantly there who seem to be fixed to the seats, it's not the kind of place where most people come for long sits. The chairs are rickety, and the wooden banquettes are good for your character — if discomfort *does* build character. But never mind, you don't have to eat the chairs.

The description of some of the food makes it sound as austere as the furniture in this vegetarian-style eatery. But the taste is fulsome: the high-protein burger doesn't need meat. It's a lovely concoction of grains, nuts, mushrooms, and herbs, which is buried in pita under melted cheese, some vegetables, and a lovely tahina sauce ($3.50). Lunch or light dinner could be a bowl of soup (these change daily and could be dill and potato, vegetable, or a chicken-soup-based lemon soup) served with a slice of the good whole wheat bread and a couple of chunks of cheddar for an extra $1.00. There are also some fresh fish specials at higher prices.

Desserts, some of which are from Dufflet Pastries, are creamy and cakey treats that will remove any feeling of deprivation you might be harboring ($2.50 to $2.95). Queen Mother is owned by some former lawyers who also own the Rivoli down the street.

---

208 Queen St. W (just west of
   University Ave.)
598-4719
Hours: 11:30 A.M. to 1 A.M. Monday to
   Saturday

Closed: Sunday; Christmas Day, Easter,
   major Jewish holidays
Licensed: Full
Payment: Visa, MasterCard
Parking: Street

THE BAMBOO CLUB

This club is loved as much for its clientele as for its food — both are entertaining. Spicy Thai noodles are stir fried with egg, chicken, shrimp, and peanuts, for $6.95. Stir-fried orange-cashew chicken comes with rice, seasonal vegetables, and gado-gado salad. Chicken or pork satay is marinated meat threaded on a bamboo skewer and grilled with a spicy peanut sauce. In the summer, the patio and treetop lounge feature barbecues in the open air. There is live entertainment nightly.

312 Queen St. W. (at Peter St.)
593-5771
Hours: Noon to 1 A.M. Monday to
  Saturday

Closed: Sunday; all major holidays
Licensed: Full
Payment: Visa, MasterCard, AmEx
Parking: Some on the street; parking lot
  one block east

THE RIVOLI

A casual and comfortable restaurant, the Rivoli is popular in the area for its ambience and entertainment. People come to eat, and just to sit at the bar and talk. The back room features changing events such as poetry readings, bands, and comedy nights. The Rivoli is owned by three former lawyers.

The spring rolls are four for $3.25 and are served with a mildly spicy sauce with peanuts and carrots; other Laotian dishes include the stir-fry dishes for $5.75 to $8.50. Try the open-faced crabmeat sandwich on dark rye with melted cheese; it's a feast for $4.25.

334 Queen St. W. (west of University Ave.)
596-1908
Hours: Noon to 1 A.M. Monday to Saturday, 5:30 P.M. to 11 P.M. Sunday

Closed: Christmas Day, Easter, major Jewish holidays
Licensed: Full
Payment: Visa
Parking: Street

BARNEY'S OPEN KITCHEN

Barney is legendary in these parts, both for his food and for his gruff friendliness. The friendliness may come and go, but the food is always the same — simple, cheap and wonderful. The French toast, for example, is soaked in eggs and milk for a while before it's grilled, so that it's like pieces of delicious custard afloat in maple syrup. The other egg dishes are well loved also. The deli sandwiches are thick and very good — especially the corned beef. Whatever it is, Barney will feed you right. This is a very small and very casual counter-and-table restaurant, which is nearly always full. It is especially popular for Saturday brunch.

385 Queen St. W. (just west of
   Spadina Ave.)
593-0713
Hours: 6:45 A.M. to 2:45 P.M. Monday
   to Friday, 6:45 A.M. to 12:45 A.M.
   Saturday

Closed: Sunday; several days at
   Christmas and New Year's
Licensed: No
Payment: Cash only
Parking: Street

ROONEEM'S BAKERY

Rooneem's is a quick cafeteria if you're in a hurry, or a neighborly place to sit and chat or think. Either way, the food is good and inexpensive. Every meal comes with sweet-sour bread, or try the double bran, which is wonderful. Breakfast of eggs, bacon, ham or sausage, coffee, and bread is available all day for $2.50 (except at lunch). Desserts include baked apple in a jacket for $1.00, or a slice of Black Forest cake for $1.50. Light falls into distinct areas in this restaurant, and owner Valdo Rooneem claims that people choose their areas as their moods dictate. One-third of the restaurant is saved for non-smokers.

484 Queen St. W. (near Bathurst St.)
366-1205
Hours: 7 A.M. to 6 P.M. Tuesday to Friday, 7 A.M. to 5 P.M. Saturday

Closed: Sunday, Monday; Christmas Day, Boxing Day, New Year's Day, Easter
Licensed: No
Payment: Cash only
Parking: In the rear; street

EPICURE CAFÉ

The Epicure Café is a very pleasant, cozy restaurant with a beautiful long bar at the back. Its prices generally are low, but those that fall most within the scope of this book for prices and quality include the generous burgers, boeuf Bourguignon and the Waldorf salad.

---

512 Queen St. W. (at Portland St.)

363-8942

Hours: 11 A.M. to 11 P.M. Monday to Thursday, 11 A.M. to 12:30 A.M. Friday, 11 A.M. to midnight Saturday, 11 A.M. to 10 P.M. Sunday

Closed: Never

Licensed: Full

Payment: Visa, MasterCard, AmEx

Parking: Street; parking lot across the street

VIENNA HOME BAKERY

Essentially a bakery, this spot is frequented as a café by loyal locals. They come to sit and enjoy rum-butter and pecan pies ($2.75), the fresh ginger cake served with a stewed pear ($2.50), or any of the seasonal fruit pies, which may include cranberry, pear, and pumpkin. You may have already marveled at the desserts in other restaurants like the Senator, Emilio's, and the Renaissance Café, which the Vienna Home Bakery supplies. Popular savory dishes include the soups served with fresh bread for $2.65. These may include black bean, minestrone, and pumpkin. On Saturday, there's a breakfast platter of eggs, bacon or sausage, homefries done in garlic and onion, and some whole wheat bread, all for $3.00. Breakfasts sometimes come cheaper, but rarely as satisfying. Bread comes out of the oven daily at noon.

626 Queen St. W. (at Markham St.)
366-1278
Hours: 9 A.M. to 6 P.M. Tuesday to
    Friday, 10 A.M. to 6 P.M. Saturday
Takeout also

Closed: Sunday, Monday; Christmas
    Day
Licensed: No
Payment: Cash only
Parking: Street

PRAGUE MEAT PRODUCTS

A warm, family-run deli with counters and stools in the rear, the Prague features the kind service, hearty food, and a comfortable atmosphere that has made it a favorite for sixteen years. Two soups are offered daily for $1.50 each: goulash soup and hot borscht. Roast-beef dinner with dumplings, potatoes or rice is $4.50. Beef roulades are sometimes served, too, and sauerkraut is always served. Note the early dinner closing.

638 Queen St. W. (near Palmerston Ave.)
364-1787
Hours: 9 A.M. to 7 P.M. Tuesday to Friday, 9 A.M. to 5 P.M. Saturday
Takeout also

Closed: Sunday, Monday; Christmas Day, New Year's Day, Easter
Licensed: No
Payment: Cash only
Parking: Street

THUMPERS

Perch yourself on one of fifteen stools here and settle in for some of the oddest and best hamburgers ever. All the hamburgers are made with a large chunk of beef, laid on a fresh kaiser with some lettuce and tomato, but let them talk you into one with cream cheese, or one with garlic, or best yet, one with cream cheese and smoked oysters. The basic hamburger is $2.35; even with toppings the price will get no higher than $3.50. Milkshakes are made the old-fashioned way — with milk and ice cream ($1.75). Don't miss out on the excellent homemade pies, especially the strawberry-rhubarb or the banana-cream.

1396 Queen St. W. (near Landsdowne Ave.)
533-7656
Hours: 10 A.M. to 9 P.M. Monday to Friday, 10 A.M. to 6 P.M. Saturday

Closed: Sunday
Licensed: No
Payment: Cash only
Parking: Street

WEST INDIAN ROTI

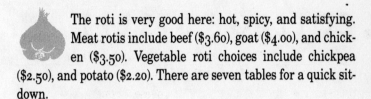 The roti is very good here: hot, spicy, and satisfying. Meat rotis include beef ($3.60), goat ($4.00), and chicken ($3.50). Vegetable roti choices include chickpea ($2.50), and potato ($2.20). There are seven tables for a quick sit-down.

1446 Queen St. W. (near Landsdowne Ave.)
532-7701
Hours: 10 A.M. to 10 P.M. Monday to Saturday
Takeout also

Closed: Statutory holidays
Licensed: No
Payment: Cash only
Parking: Street

COLLEGE STREET

This area is a "must" for eaters. Each block west from Bathurst Street is studded with eateries that have earned their stripes for years of serving good, inexpensive food. The Clinton Street area is particularly rich in this regard. Within a few blocks are several places that serve excellent hot veal sandwiches and good pizza. And take some time on a Saturday to poke through the many Italian food shops, where you'll find bargains in specialty meats, cheeses, and olives. There are some good shops for fresh fish as well. Look for Mediterannean varieties that are hard to come by elsewhere.

On hot summer evenings, join the throngs for espresso and homemade ices in any of the small bars that dot this street.

MASSIMO PIZZA & PASTA

You've probably driven by this place and wondered about it — it's very colorful, small, and very busy. What it is, is a pizza phenomenon. In its 3½ years of operation, Massimo's has appeared on many lists of the best pizza places in town. Surprisingly then, the most popular order isn't for the pizza, but for the calzone. This is much like a pizza turnover — a large round piece of dough is folded over savory fillings like seafood, pesto, or standard pizza toppings, and baked. It is something like a panzarotto, except that a panzarotto is fried. The result is delicious and costs about $4.00, depending on the filling. The pizza is special partly because of the offbeat toppings, such as pesto and seafood. A plain medium (14-inch) pizza is $6.50. It's 75 cents a topping after that.

302 College St. (just west of Spadina Ave.)

967-0527

Hours: Noon to 1 A.M. Monday to Thursday, Noon to 2 A.M. Friday, Saturday, Noon to midnight Sunday

Closed: Christmas Day, Easter

Licensed: No

Payment: Cash only

Parking: Street

FREE TIMES CAFÉ

Free Times is a homey sort of place with nice, inexpensive food, all made on the premises. Customers, many of whom are in social services and the arts, come for the camaraderie and the live entertainment, but mostly for the applecrisp pie ($2.95). There is always a vegetarian special like vegetarian lasagna ($5.25 with salad). Shrimp mignonette is shrimp stir fried in curry butter with Pernod ($5.50). Sunday brunch (11:30 A.M. to 4 P.M.) costs about $5.00.

320 College St. (west of Spadina Ave.)
967-1078
Hours: 11:30 A.M. to 1 A.M. Monday to
   Saturday, 11:30 A.M. to midnight
   Sunday

Closed: Christmas Day, Boxing Day
Licensed: Full
Payment: Visa, MasterCard, AmEx
Parking: Street

VIETNAM RESTAURANT

 Meals served in this three-year-old family restaurant are made particularly notable by the very fresh ingredients that are used. Owners Kim Ma and Jim Ngo shop in Kensington Market just before they open at 4 P.M. for the vegetables and seafood that end up in such dishes as water blue (garlic, onion, scallops, shrimp, and squid served on a sizzling hot plate), the pineapple pot of shrimp curry served in a pineapple shell, and many others. The water blue and pineapple pot are $8.50 and $8.00 respectively, and each is big enough for two people. Spring rolls with beef, or the imperial rolls with shrimp salad served with peanut sauce, are $2.50.

338 College St. (near Augusta Ave.)
922-2271
Hours: 4 P.M. to 1 A.M. seven days

Closed: Never
Licensed: No
Payment: Cash only
Parking: Street

MARS RESTAURANT

The sign outside promises food that's "out of this world," but it's more that the Mars itself belongs to some rare world where food is reliable, prices are good, and service is fast and friendly. An old-fashioned diner, the Mars' twenty-five stools and nine tables are always full at prime times, usually with customers who wouldn't think of eating their meals anywhere else. There's often a lineup at the cash register of people who have come to take out the famous Mars muffins. Among the favorite meals served is corned beef hash, a special on Saturdays and Sundays, which includes a fried egg, wonderful homefries, cole slaw, and bread for $4.00. Cheese blintzes are served with sour cream and applesauce for $4.20. There's nothing fancy about the breakfasts, except that they're good. The rice pudding is among the creamiest and tastiest in the city. The menu is enormous but, so far, everything has been fine. The staff must think so, too: Frank has been there for thirty years, Doreen and Pearl for twenty, Jimmy for fourteen, Kim for ten, and Bill for seven.

432 College St. W. (near Bathurst St.)
921-6332
Hours: 6 A.M. to midnight seven days

Closed: Never
Licensed: No
Payment: Visa, MasterCard
Parking: Street

SOL DE ESPANA

Stop by this small shop to buy one empanada and you'll take home a dozen. Empanadas are a South American specialty, a smallish turnover filled with spicy meat, potatoes, egg, and at least one olive. They're very good at Sol De Espana, and cost $1.30 each.

468 College St. (near Bathurst St.)
960-3367
Hours: 9 A.M. to 8:30 P.M. Monday to
Saturday, 9 A.M. to 6 P.M. Sunday
Takeout only

Closed: Christmas Day, Easter
Licensed: No
Payment: Cash only
Parking: Street

BONZO'S TAKEOUT FOODS

 Bonzo's has been named as having the best burgers in town. Certainly they are among the largest — five ounces plus of ground beef served with a choice of toppings on an egg bun for $2.30. Toppings include garlic and hot peppers, so this is no wimpy patty. Kwinter hot dogs also are available $1.80, $2.35 for Kwinter's chunky style.

586 College St. (near Clinton St.)
534-8317
Hours: Winter 11 A.M. to 9 P.M.
Monday to Thursday, 11 A.M. to 10
P.M. Friday, Saturday, Summer: 11
A.M. to 11 P.M. Monday to
Saturday
Takeout only

Closed: Sunday; statutory holidays
Licensed: No
Payment: Cash only
Parking: Municipal lot nearby

SAN FRANCESCO FOODS

This 39-year-old spot is the original location of San Francesco's, the source from which sprang the many others that dot the city and bring hot veal sandwiches to the masses. The veal sandwiches here at the original location are, logically, better than those served at the branches. The sandwiches come sweet, medium, and hot, the degree of spiciness controlled by the number of hot peppers inside. Of the veal, steak, and pork sausage sandwiches, I prefer the veal ($2.50), although the sausage ($2.25) is a close second.

This is a family-run business with an atmosphere provided by generations of familiar customers, most from Italy, who come to eat or just to sit and talk in the private back room. The talking and eating start early and go late.

10 Clinton St. (south of College St., midway between Bathurst and Shaw Sts.)
534-7867
Hours: 7 A.M. to 12.30 A.M. Monday to Thursday, 7 A.M. to 3 A.M. Friday, Saturday, 8.30 A.M. to 1 P.M. Sunday
Takeout only

Closed: Christmas Day, Easter
Licensed: No
Payment: Cash only
Parking: Street

BITONDO SNACK BAR & PIZZERIA

A tiny, modest shop with a few chairs and fewer arborite tables, a Wurlitzer that plays Italian and English hits, a cold-drink cooler that takes up the space where two more tables might fit, and the best pizza in the area. The place is a local tradition and landmark, and on summer evenings you can stand at the window with the neighborhood kids and watch the cook assembling the food. The pizza is wonderful, huge, with generous toppings, and costs about $10 for a deluxe. The pizza can be bought by the piece too, a good way to start since a piece will satisfy most normal gluttons. Toppings are 40 cents extra.

It took me a while to get around to the pizza, because for many years I have busied myself with the hot veal sandwiches ($2.50). It's Mama's fresh sauce that makes these special, along with the generous pieces of breaded veal and the hot peppers. They take a long time to eat, and they're very messy, so don't go in fancy dress.

Note that Bitondo's, like San Francesco's across the street, opens early. By 9 A.M. you could be eating your first pizza or hot sandwich of the day, leaving the rest of the city to face the morning with only granola for company. Bitondo's is not licensed, but the Monarch Tavern, just across the street, is accustomed to escapees from crowded Bitondo's, and cheerfully provides a beer to go with the food you've brought.

11 Clinton St. (south of College St., midway between Bathurst and Shaw Sts.)

533-4101

Hours: 9 A.M. to 12:30 A.M. Monday to Thursday, 9 A.M. to 1 A.M. Friday, Saturday, 10 A.M. to midnight Sunday

Takeout also

Closed: Christmas Day, New Year's Day, Easter

Licensed: No

Payment: Cash only

Parking: Street

CALIFORNIA SANDWICHES

The newcomer on the block that houses Bitondo's and San Francesco's had to be good to survive. This tiny, wonderful place is run by twelve members of the same family. It's called California Sandwiches because the family thought the name had a nice ring to it, not because they serve anything from that sunny place. What they serve is just fine, if you can get there to find out. As one fan reported "This isn't one of the easiest places to find, but then, neither are pearls." It's on a little side street a block south of Bitondo's. Enter through the side door. There are small tables in a big room but, weather favoring, most people eat outside or take their sandwiches into the nearby Monarch Tavern and order a beer.

The hot veal and sausage sandwiches are huge. Sauce drips from the huge kaiser buns, made by the bakery just down the road. The veal sandwiches are the crowd's favorites, if you can judge by the random wall scrawls of the sports figures and politicians who've eaten here. The highest compliment is in a letter from the city's detective department, framed and hung on the wall.

The steak sandwich isn't special in size or taste, but the sausage one is. The sausage is homemade by Mama in the back, who also makes the sauces. Veal or steak sandwiches are $2.94 including tax; sausage sandwiches are $2.47, including tax. Just these sandwiches and soft drinks are served here, but why would you need anything more?

244 Claremont St. (take Clinton St. south off College to the end, jog left to Claremont St.)

366-3317

Hours: 9:30 A.M. to midnight Sunday to Thursday, 9:30 A.M. to 1 P.M. Friday, Saturday

Takeout also

Closed: Christmas Day, New Year's Day, Easter

Licensed: No

Payment: Cash only

Parking: Street only. There's not much legal parking, but there's a fair turnover of cars, so you should be able to find something.

BAR DIPLOMATICO
& RESTAURANT

 For nearly twenty years, the Diplomatico has been known for its cappuccino and espresso. Homemade ice cream is served here also, as it is in many of the Italian coffee stops along the street. At the Diplomatico, customers usually order the hazelnut and almond ice creams. The pizza ($4.00 for a plain medium) and panzarotto ($1.65 plain) are pretty good too.

594 College St. (west of Bathurst St.)
534-4637
Hours: 8 A.M. to 2 A.M. Monday to
  Saturday, 8 A.M. to midnight
  Sunday

Closed: Christmas Day, Easter
Licensed: Full
Payment: Cash only
Parking: Parking lot in back; street

BRAZIL PORTUGUESE BUTCHER

This is a small corner grocery store that cooks up grilled chicken halves over flames that lick the skin and meat until they're salty and spicy, soft and sweet. It's about the best grilled chicken around ($5.50 for the whole bird — ask for two halves). The chicken is available on a take-out basis only. The grilled chicken is to be distinguished from the barbecued chicken, which is roasted whole on a spit and is good too. The grilled chicken must be ordered in advance because it takes about half an hour to cook. Take home a few of the bread rolls and, if it's the right season, some fresh corn will make for a super meal.

705 College St. (near Montrose Ave.)
531-1120
Hours: Approximately 8 or 9 A.M. to
    about 7 to 9 P.M. seven days
Takeout only

Closed: Christmas Day, New Year's Day
Licensed: No
Payment: Cash only
Parking: Street

SICILIAN ICE CREAM CO. LTD.

Torontonians have been "discovering" this ice cream parlor for twenty-six years. It is a large, open restaurant with outdoor seating in the summer, located in a busy area where there's lots to watch. Ice cream is served in three-scoop servings for $2.25, and include all the ordinary flavors, as well as banana, coffee, nut, and lemon. Spumoni, cassata, and tartufo also cost $2.25 a serving. Espresso and cappuccino are available as well. This is a family business that supplies ice cream to many restaurants in southern Ontario.

712 College St. (near Montrose Ave.)
531-7716
Hours: 10 A.M. to midnight Monday to
Thursday, 10 A.M. to 1 A.M. Friday,
Saturday, Sunday

Closed: Early closings only at
Christmas, and New Year's
Licensed: No
Payment: Cash only
Parking: Street

BLOOR STREET WEST

T he chunk of Bloor Street that runs west between Bathurst and Jane streets has quietly been gathering gastronomic speed over the last few years. Just west of Bathurst, there are several Korean restaurants that serve spicy, good food. More recently, Indonesian and Malaysian restaurants have been added. Farther west, near High Park, is a section of Bloor that is packed with bakeries, and cheese and sausage shops, most with a middle-European flavor. Spend a Saturday here just before Christmas or Easter, when the shops are overflowing with special holiday treasures.

SOUTHERN ACCENT

 Owned and operated by the folks who have successfully established the By The Way Café and the Rosedale Diner, this newest addition serves up the flaming trend in American regional food — creole. Located on a festive street, Southern Accent serves good food such as mussels creolewitz, which is mussels in a spicy creole sauce ($4.95 and $8.95). Blackened fresh fish is Southern Accent's interpretation of blackened redfish, one of the best dishes of Louisiana cookery. The fish is coated with sixteen spices and dry fried. Jambalaya is a huge dish of rice with shrimp and okra, zipped with creole sauce. Don't miss the baked garlic appetizer. Squeeze a clove on a piece of bread, spread it and eat with a piece of feta cheese.

595 Markham St. (south of Bloor St. W.)
536-3211
Hours: 5 P.M. to 11 P.M. Monday to Thursday, Noon to 11 P.M. Saturday, Sunday

Closed: Christmas Day, New Year's Day
Licensed: Full
Payment: Visa, MasterCard, AmEx
Parking: Parking lot in back

RASA RIA

 Billed as a Malaysian-Singapore restaurant, the Rasa Ria's interior is casual, yet respectable, with tablecloths and placemats, carpeting, and candles.

The best menu so far has been pie tee (known to regulars as "Thai pie"), small, hot, crisply corrugated pastry cups shaped like top hats and filled with a mixture of crab, shrimp, shredded carrot, and other vegetables — a filling reminiscent of a spring roll. Each one is a full mouthful, so order as many mouthfuls as you can handle before what will be a satisfying meal ($2.95 buys a serving of four).

Goreng ikan is fish (usually grouper or pickerel) with ginger, marinated in tumeric and other spices, then pan fried and served with a ginger sauce ($7.35). The resulting flavor and presentation make it special. Goreng ayam sayur is stir-fried chicken breast, sautéed with vegetables and cashew nuts ($6.75). Ask for specials and watch the dishes traveling to other tables. Many of the dishes are mildly spicy. The service is kind, and advice is freely given in this warm, family-run restaurant.

---

615 Bloor St. W. (near Palmerston Blvd.)

532-1632

Hours: Noon to 3 P.M. and 5 P.M. to 11 P.M. Monday to Thursday, Noon to 3 P.M. and 5 P.M. to 11:30 P.M. Friday, Saturday, 5 P.M. to 11:30 P.M. Sunday

Closed: All major holidays

Licensed: Beer and wine

Payment: Visa, AmEx, Diners Club, MasterCard

Parking: Street; lot nearby

KOREA HOUSE RESTAURANT

Korea House has been an established and reliable restaurant for over fifteen years, and was respected long before Torontonians learned to feel safe with very spicy foods. Among the most popular dishes is the bul goki beef, marinated first in a delicious soy-sesame sauce and cooked on a hot griddle at the table. A dinner that includes soup, rice, marinated seasonal vegetables and kim chee costs $9.00. Kalbi ribs is a beef rib that is sliced flat and thin, marinated and then barbecued in a special sauce (full dinner costs $9.00). Bibim bat is a bowlful of rice topped with marinated beef, a fried egg, several varieties of marinated vegetables, and an exciting hot sauce, a meal for about $6.00. There is a sushi bar at the back of the restaurant, featuring a few very offbeat dishes like the one with raw beef, pine nuts, and pears.

666 Bloor St. W.
536-8666
Hours: Noon to 1 A.M. seven days

Closed: Never
Licensed: Full
Payment: Visa, MasterCard
Parking: Street

SATAY-SATAY RESTAURANT

Satay is a delightful snack of marinated meat, or seafood, skewered on bamboo, grilled, and served with a spicy peanut sauce. It is sold by street vendors in Thailand, and at this pleasant, reasonably priced Thai restaurant. Start with that, then try the pom yum king, lemon shrimp soup ($1.65 a bowl at lunch; $4.95 at dinner for a large pot which feeds two), or the mussels flavored with coconut sauce. A good selection of main meals is available, many very spicy and most flavored with coriander. Phad Thai, which is rice noodles stir fried with chicken, shrimp, and vegetables, is among the most popular ($5.65), and the whole fish in sweet and sour sauce is also wonderful.

700 Bloor St. W. (near Christie St.)
532-7489
Hours: Lunch: Phone first to check if lunches available, Dinner: 4:30 P.M. to 10:30 P.M. Sunday to Thursday, 4:30 P.M. to 11 P.M. Friday, Saturday

Closed: Thanksgiving, Christmas Day, New Year's Day
Licensed: Yes
Payment: Visa, MasterCard, AmEx
Parking: Municipal lot at back

EQUINOCCIAL

An Equadorian restaurant that serves huge offbeat-sounding platters of food, which is just plain good family fare. Ceviche is marinated raw seafood, "cooked" by the acidic lemon and lime juices of the marinade. The humita is corn meal and cheese wrapped in a corn leaf, and it's wonderful. The empanandas are lightly sprinkled with sugar so they taste a bit like a dessert fritter. And those are just the appetizers.

For your main course, try churrasco, a platter of beef, eggs, shredded lettuce, and potato, for $6.oo. Shrimp in garlic is $8.oo. Get it for wonderful garlic taste and a plate filled with shrimp, rice, and potatoes. Most of the platters include toasted yellow corn or boiled white corn, or both. Whatever else you order, ask for the garlic potatoes with peanut sauce. It's not on the menu but will be made on request. And, if they're available, the tongue stew and lamb stew, tripe, and cowfoot soup are also popular.

This is a licensed and comfortable restaurant by this guide's standards. There are tablecloths and placemats, bona fide table service, and even entertainment on Saturday nights.

---

814 Bloor St. W. (near Crawford St.)
536-6956
Hours: 11 A.M. to 11 P.M. Wednesday
    to Monday

Closed: Tuesday; open on holidays,
    unless these fall on a Tuesday
Licensed: Full
Payment: Visa, MasterCard
Parking: Street

GREEK ISLANDS RESTAURANT

Lamb and pork roast on a spit in the window, and inside is a large room with plenty of tables where you can have some good and hearty Greek food for not very much money. A small skewer of grilled meat costs $1.00. The same meat in a large bun, with lots of tzadziki and some onions and tomatoes, makes a meal. The roast lamb dinner includes salad and roast potatoes; it costs $7.50 and will feed two. Pork souvlaki served with Greek salad, rice, roast potatoes, tzadziki, and bread and butter, is $5.95. There are restaurants like the Greek Islands at the other end of Bloor Street, on the Danforth, but if you're in this neighborhood, you can save yourself a trip.

888 Bloor St. W. (near Ossington Ave.)   Closed: Never
537-0666   Licensed: Full
Hours 8 A.M. to 2 A.M. Monday to   Payment: Visa
   Saturday, 8 A.M. to midnight   Parking: Street; parking lot behind
   Sunday

PARADISE SWEETS & SNACKS

Paradise, in this case, means inexpensive and good Indian food. Meat curries are priced at $3.25, and there is a reasonable selection of vegetable dishes and breads as well. A special dish called thali is made up of several kinds of curry, and served with rice, bread, and salad for $3.50. Paradise also has a large selection of Indian sweets. The restaurant is small (seven tables) and very casual.

1015 Bloor St. W. (near Rusholme Rd.)
536-2244
Hours: 11:30 A.M. to 11:30 P.M.
   Wednesday to Monday

Closed: Tuesday
Licensed: Full
Payment: Visa
Parking: Street

PENANG ISLAND RESTAURANT

Penang Island specializes in the foods of Malaysia and Singapore, with the emphasis on seafood dishes. All of the dishes are prepared by the owner-cook Meng Heng. The most popular meals include the assam redang sambal (seafood in a tomato sauce flavored with coconut, tamarind, onion, garlic and sweet peppers ($7.95); mussels pan fried with chilies, garlic, onion, tomato sauce, brandy, and peanuts ($8.95); and beef prepared with ginger, coconut, and chilies ($5.95). It is a small restaurant with about nine tables.

1546 Bloor St. W. (near Dufferin St.)
534-0461
Hours: 3 P.M. to midnight Tuesday to
   Thursday, Noon to midnight Friday
   to Sunday

Closed: Monday
Licensed: Beer and wine
Payment: Visa, MasterCard
Parking: Street

THE GOLDEN EMBERS

The Golden Embers is a favorite breakfast spot for people who live in the area. There is nothing much to recommend the decor, but definitely recommended is the hearty breakfast of a selection of eggs, corned-beef hash, sausage, peameal bacon, ham, toast, and coffee. It costs $2.65 if you have it between 7 A.M. and 11 A.M., $3.15 if you sleep in and don't get there until after 11. The restaurant closes at 2 P.M. There are hamburgers for $1.75 and a daily soup and special, too, but it's breakfast that people talk about.

1730 Bloor St. W. (near Keele St.)
763-3666
Hours: 7 A.M. to 2 P.M. seven days

Closed: Christmas Day, New Year's Day
Licensed: No
Payment: Cash only
Parking: Street

CONTINENTAL FLAIR
DINING LOUNGE

Watch for daily specials in this comfortable restaurant. These are priced from $2.95 to $6.95. The regular menu has equally low prices; beef bordelaise (pan-fried beef medallions) is $5.95, while a meal of filet mignon tips served with Caesar salad is $6.95. In addition, seven specials priced from $2.95 to $6.95 are on the menu board each day. Portions are adequate and the flavors are fine.

2350 Dundas St. W. (near Bloor St. intersection)
535-0547
Hours: 11 A.M. to 11 P.M. seven days

Closed: Christmas Day
Licensed: Full
Payment: Visa, MasterCard, AmEx
Parking: Underground

GRENADIER RESTAURANT
HIGH PARK

This is a wonderfully inexpensive restaurant in an interesting location that's well worth finding. Breakfasts, for example, are $1.95 for three eggs, peameal bacon, plus the usuals. Shish kebab is $3.50 in the coffee shop, and a meal of liver and onions is $4.50 in the dining room with soup and coffee, and only $2.95 if you'll settle for it in the coffee shop. The menu is huge and includes cabbage rolls, stuffed peppers, and corned beef on a kaiser. Everything is homemade by the Caragianatos.

200 Parkside Dr. (in the middle of High Park)
769-9870
Hours: Summer: 7 A.M. to 10 P.M. seven days, Winter: Closes at 8 P.M. Nov. 1 to May 1

Closed: Never
Licensed: No
Payment: Cash only
Parking: Huge parking lot in front

ST. CLAIR
AVENUE WEST

Take a long walk on a Saturday afternoon along St. Clair Avenue from Bathurst Street west to Dufferin and beyond. This street has blossomed with clothing shops and restaurants, most of them Italian. Espresso and ice cream bars and pizzerias and places for hot veal sandwiches abound. A few health food stores and health-minded restaurants also have been added to the mix in recent years.

The increasing number of full-service Italian restaurants range from very casual to expensive — as do all of the businesses on this constantly changing street. Stop in at some of these restaurants as you explore the spiffy clothing stores offering the latest from Milan. Café Romeo is shiny and well-established; the Venezia on Lansdowne Avenue has long been loved for its fresh pasta; the Tre Mari Bakery has a deli counter that is open 24 hours a day. Saturday afternoons and summer evenings are the street's busiest times.

Much further west, near Jane Street, are Santino's Bakery and Scarlett Italian Bakery. Both are on Scarlett Street just off St. Clair. These bakeries have a retinue of fans who wouldn't let a week go by without their buns, meats and cheeses, usually assembled and eaten on the spot.

FATSO'S HOMEMADE HAMBURGERS & ICE CREAM PARLOUR

Don't ask for just a hamburger in this place — you'll be corrected and told that they don't have just hamburgers here, but "homemade hamburgers." This overly lit hamburger bar is particularly popular among the high-school set. The format is something like Lick's and Harvey's: order at the counter, then sit down while your food's being cooked on a grill. When your number's called you stand in front of the counter again to tell the happy kid behind it what you want on your homemade hamburger — the wide array of toppings includes all the usual pickles and relishes, plus a few extras like hot peppers. The hamburgers (from $2.45) are thick and good. The french fries are fine; coney fries have chili on them. The onion rings are huge and very doughy, but very good if you like batter. There are unusual flavors of pretty good ice cream, including Tiger.

536 St. Clair Ave. W. (near Bathurst St.)
654-9233
Hours: 11 A.M.to midnight Monday to Thursday, 11 A.M. to 2 A.M. Friday, Saturday, 11:30 A.M. to 11 P.M. Sunday

Closed: Christmas Day, New Year's Day
Licensed: No
Payment: Cash only
Parking: Parking lot in front

LEDLOW'S

If you let some creative kids mix up concoctions of their own, you'd get things like Ledlow's Hellava Thing, which is a mishmash of hash browns, avocado, onions, cheese, and barbecue sauce. The sauce is a bit sweet and the combination is appalling — but it works. Served in a bowl, with toast made from their wonderful homemade bread, it looks like chili but tastes like the best things kids ever liked, all rolled into one. The Special Thing (for a bit more money) is the same thing only with fried fresh mushrooms. The wonderful bread makes the Monte Cristo sandwich special, three layers of cheese and turkey — so good.

Part of Ledlow's charm is that the menu and approach changes from time to time, so that what's wonderful this month may not be there next month. We hope, though, that the chocolate cheesecake and the paradise salad made with salt cod, avocado, and green onions are still there the next time.

If you ask if things are homemade, the waiter will answer: "We make everything here except the carpet and the wine." The owners are two escapees from the downtown Pickle Barrel who thought they could do fine on their own. They can.

---

682 St. Clair Ave. W. (at Christie St.)
656-8646
Hours: Noon to 10 P.M. Monday to
   Saturday

Closed: Sunday
Licensed: Full
Payment: Visa, AmEx
Parking: Street

OLE MALACCA

Pronounced "ole" as in "hole", (never "olay,") this charming, family-run restaurant opened to great acclaim about four years ago, in a part of the city then better known for cappuccino bars than for the Singapore-Malaysian fare that Ole Malacca did so well. The area has changed since then, and so has Ole Malacca. Its popularity seems to have affected it somewhat — spicy dishes seem less spicy and exotic foods seem less so. Nevertheless, Ole Malacca remains a very pleasant place for a good meal, and sometimes it hits the "ole" heights.

For appetizers, have the satay, which is marinated chunks of chicken, shrimps and pork skewered on a bamboo rod and grilled at the table ($4.95). The satay is served with a slightly spicy, slightly sweet peanut sauce. The dinner menu is extensive and you may wish to ask for guidance from the waiter. Among the offerings is Ole Malacca Lala, a wonderful platter of fresh mussels that have been stir fried with chunks of peanuts in a sambal (chili) sauce ($8.95). Most of the seafood dishes are exceptional. Try too the hot plate, made up of prawns that have been marinated and set to sizzle on a very hot platter. The prawns are served with a chilic sauce made with brandy. Combine the two for a hot and happy plateful of juicy prawns ($10.95).

888 St. Clair Ave. W. (near Winona
  Dr.)
654-2111
– and –
67 Shuter St. (near Church St.)
364-2400
Hours: 5 P.M. to 11 P.M. Monday to
  Saturday

Closed: Sundays; Thanksgiving Day,
  Christmas Day
Licensed: Full
Payment: Visa, AmEx, all major cards
Parking: Street

SIDEWALK RESTAURANT & TAVERN

Run by two men who are both named Tony (Tesone and Henriques), the Sidewalk has been popular in the area for many years, maintaining a loyal clientele that doesn't seem to mind that the style of Italian food has changed somewhat. It is a fairly large restaurant with an attached banquet room. Prices are moderate, and the food is quite good. Pasta with seafood costs $6.95; saltimbocca, a large dish of veal with cheese and prosciutto, is less common these days and is offered here for $9.50. Service is friendly.

1662 Dufferin St. (just south of St. Clair Ave. W.)

654-9725

Hours: 11:30 A.M. to 11 P.M. Monday to Wednesday, 11:30 A.M. to 1 A.M. Friday, Saturday

Takout also

Closed: Sunday; Christmas Day, New Year's Day

Licensed: Full

Parking: At rear; on street

LA BRUSCHETTA

This is a small, fifteen-table, family-oriented restaurant that serves good regional Italian food at medium prices. It is named for that cunning little appetizer of Italian bread, spread with olive oil, and grilled with chunks of fresh tomato and parmesan cheese that seems so simple and tastes so good. Of the main meals, the seafood platter is probably the most popular dish: a huge meal of clams, shrimp, baby shark, and Alaskan crab, cooked in a tomato sauce, and served with spaghetti and salad. It is made only for two or more people and costs $25 for two. The pastas are made on the premises and are quite good, especially the fettuccine capricciosa, which is spinach noodles cooked in a tomato and cream sauce with olives, ham, and some herbs ($7.00). A favorite that is not listed on the menu — but which can be had with some pleading — is the spaghetti alla pescadore, which is spaghetti in a white sauce with cuttlefish, clams, and mussels. Ask Benny, the owner, about it.

1325 St. Clair Ave. W. (near Dufferin St.)
656-8622
Hours: Noon to 3 P.M.; 5 P.M. to 11 P.M. Monday to Friday, Noon to 3 P.M.; 5 P.M. to midnight Saturday

Closed: Sunday; all major holidays
Licensed: Full
Payment: Visa, AmEx, MasterCard
Parking: Street

SALOIYA RESTAURANT

This is a small, family restaurant run by a father and daughter, which serves good Indian food for low prices. Chicken pikka is $4.95; goat boona is $5.95, and spinach-cheese palak paneer is $2.50. There are a lot of other dishes that Dad will advise you on and then bring to your table. Decor is non-existent, but the service is friendly.

3345 Dundas St. W. (near Runnymead Rd.)

766-0561

Hours: 11:30 A.M. to 9 P.M. Monday to Friday, 2 P.M. to 8 P.M. Saturday and Sunday

Closed: Never

Licensed: No

Payment: Cash only

Parking: Street

VESUVIO'S PIZZERIA & SPAGHETTI HOUSE

 Vesuvio's has been praised several times as having the best pizza in town, and it is, in fact, a wonderful pizza. A medium (14-inch) plain pizza costs $6.75, and toppings are 50 cents each. Lasagna and gnocchi are listed too, but Vesuvio's does best with pizza.

3014 Dundas St. W. (near High Park)
763-4191
Hours: 4 P.M. to 1 A.M. Monday to
   Thursday, 11 A.M. to 2 A.M. Friday,
   Saturday, 3 P.M. to midnight Sunday
Takeout and delivery also

Closed: Christmas
Licensed: No
Payment: Visa
Parking: Street

FRONT STREET / ST. LAWRENCE MARKET

Because of its compelling attraction for tourists and its proximity to downtown, this area has more than its share of expensive restaurants, though some diligence reveals an underground of bargains. These are easy to find in the summer, when chip wagons and food vendors line the streets. Don't miss the chip wagons at Harbourfront — the chips are fat and wonderful.

Year-round, the St. Lawrence Market is a treasure trove for food bargain-hunters. Once destined for the wrecker's ball, this great indoor market has undergone an enormous revival, and gets more lively every year. Come for the take-home goodies like meats, seafood, cheese, and produce by all means, but while you're at it, check out the stalls in the south market that sell ready-to-eat food. The best of these reflect the best of the market — sausage sandwiches, peameal bacon burgers, and such. The richness of the market fertilizes the surrounding areas, too, so there are many small places for a quick bite. Coasters, across the street from the south market and upstairs from the Old Fish Market, is a comfortable spot for a beer and fresh oysters.

GRAN FESTA RISTORANTE

A refreshing throwback to how Italian food in Toronto used to be before it got chic is this thoroughly decorated restaurant, which offers a nine-course Italian dinner — everything from antipasto to figs and coffee — for $13.95. Live music, painted ceramics, and lots of rusticity contribute to the mood.

The daily special costs $4.50, and may be braised lamb or cannelloni served with salad. The Gran Festa offers lower prices for children on the big dinners and, with all the frou-frou this is definitely a kid's kind of place.

---

146 Front St. W. (just west of
   University Ave.)
979-2020
Hours: 11:30 A.M. to 1 A.M. Sunday to
   Friday, 4:30 P.M. to 1 A.M. Saturday

Closed: Christmas Day, New Year's Day
Licensed: Full
Payment: Visa, MasterCard, enRoute
Parking: Parking lots, east and west

HUGHIE'S BURGERS, FRIES & PIES

Hughie's is a casually beautiful restaurant, and a comfortable place to leisurely enjoy a hamburger and a beer. The name of the restaurant tells you what's best here. Of the burgers, try the lamburger first, then the pizza, taco, or bacon-and-cheese burgers. All come with fries (the sweet potato fries are really special). There is a wide variety of pies, including banana-cream, chocolate-marble mousse, and peanut butter. Hughie's is named for co-owner Hugh Garber, who left fashion design for food in 1983. The restaurant is kitty-corner from the O'Keefe Centre.

22 Front St. W. (near Yonge St.)
364-2242
Hours: 11:30 A.M. to 11:30 P.M.
   Monday, Tuesday, 11:30 A.M.to 1
   A.M. Wednesday to Saturday, Noon
   to 10 P.M. Sunday

Closed: Statutory holidays
Licensed: Full
Payment: Visa, MasterCad, AmEx,
   enRoute
Parking: Some on street; parking lot on
   east side

CAROUSEL BAKERY & SANDWICH BAR

Walk to the back of the south market, past the cheeses, past the fish and the windows of meat, to find food that's all ready to eat on the spot. The Carousel has been in the market for fifty years, serving hot meat sandwiches. The most popular is the peameal bacon on a bun (usually a kaiser roll, but you have a choice of breads) for $2.30 including tax. Also loved is the spicy, hot sausage on a bun for $2.15, or the hot roast-beef sandwiches ($3.00). You can perch at a counter and eat it there, or walk around. The sandwiches are very satisfying and may help you to feel less tempted to buy everything you see in the market.

93 Front St. E. (in the St. Lawrence Market)
363-4247
Hours: 8 A.M. to 6 P.M. Tuesday to Thursday, 8 A.M. to 7 P.M. Friday, 5 A.M. to 5 P.M. Saturday

Closed: Sunday, Monday; all statutory holidays
Licensed: No
Payment: Cash only
Parking: Nearby parking lots

CROOKS RESTAURANT BAR

Actor Dan Ackroyd is a partner in this good-sized downtown roadhouse. Crooks serves especially good Buffalo-style chicken wings, regularly priced at $4.95, half-price on Tuesday nights. Also try the burgers, with fries and salad, for $4.95 to $5.75. The Billy Club is a different kind of sandwich — chicken and cheddar cheese are wrapped in smoked ham, breaded and fried — a tasty morsel for $3.75.

106 Front St. E. (near Jarvis St.)
365-8906
Hours: Noon to 1 A.M. Monday to
    Saturday, Noon to 11 P.M. Sunday

Closed: All statutory holidays
Licensed: Full
Payment: Visa, AmEx
Parking: Street; municipal lot nearby

DOWNTOWN

This is a very broad area that includes restaurants south of Bloor Street, north of King Street, just west of the Don Valley Parkway, and east of Bathurst Street.

Traditionally, downtown was where people worked, not lived, but the downtown area has become increasingly residential and some restaurants stay open late because of it. Still, gems are few and far between, but they *are* there, often in unexpected places.

The Yonge Street strip between Bloor and Front streets is lined with fast food places that run the gamut from corporate junk food to little mama and papa homemade food stands. And don't miss the terrific hot dogs to be had in the diner in Simpson's basement.

CIAO ESPRESSO BAR

Pasta is the specialty in this cheerfully decorated, inexpensive restaurant. That combination has made Ciao a popular restaurant in this location and in its newer spot at 551 Bloor Street West. In both locations, Ciao competes with a great many restaurants. The most popular dishes include the da Vinci, fettuccine with clams, shrimps, and tomato sauce ($5.50), and the veal and meatball dishes (both at $5.25 for the dinner).

534 Church St. (near Wellesley St. E.)
928-3222
Hours: 11 A.M. to 1 A.M. Monday to
    Friday, Noon to 1 A.M. Saturday,
    Noon to midnight Sunday

Closed: Christmas Day
Licensed: Beer and wine
Payment: Visa, MasterCard, AmEx,
    Diners Club
Parking: Some on street; underground
    lot

WENDY'S CATERING & TAKEOUT

 There is no set menu here and nowhere to sit, which is just what the local lunchers seem to want. They come to carry away Wendy's egg-and-shrimp, chicken-and-leek, and roast-meat sandwiches, all generously filled for $2.50. The variety of savory pies available includes ham-and-pear, beef-and-oyster-mushroom, and empanada for $2.50 to $3.00 per slice. Quiche choices include spinach and tomato, and curried cauliflower. Call ahead if you want something special.

525 Queen St. E. (near River St.)
366-3413
Hours: 8:30 A.M. to 3 P.M. Monday to
  Friday
Takeout only

Closed: Saturday, Sunday; statutory
  holidays
Licensed: No
Payment: Cash only
Parking: Street

STELLA'S PIZZA

There's nothing much to say about the pizza made by owners John Stella and his mother Margaret, except that it's terrific and reasonably priced. A plain medium pizza is $5.75, and toppings are 75 cents extra. Other homemade offerings include veal sandwiches, fettuccine, lasagna, and gnocchi. Takeout and delivery.

739 Queen St. E. (near Lewis St.)
469-5121
Hours: 11:30 A.M. to 11 P.M. Monday
to Thursday, 11:30 A.M. to 2 A.M.
Friday and Saturday, 4 P.M. to 11
P.M. Sunday

Closed: Christmas Day, New Year's
Day, Easter
Licensed: No
Payment: Cash only
Parking: Street

MR. FARROUGE

Open for only a few years, this spot quickly became well known for its falafel, and for good reason. The sandwiches are thick, dripping with sauce, and flavorful ($2.25). Other specials include a generous donair ($2.95) and shish kebab ($2.95). Its ten tables seat forty, so finding a seat inside is easy, especially during off hours. Finding a place to park is more of a challenge, since there is very little parking in the area and parking tickets come fast in this well-patrolled strip. Since the cost of the parking ticket will raise the price of the falafel beyond reasonable bounds, takeout is the solution. Owner Eddie understands and will fill your order quickly.

355½ Yonge St. (north of Dundas St. W.)
596-0479
Hours: 10 A.M. to 1 A.M. seven days
Takeout also

Closed: Never
Licensed: No
Payment: Cash only
Parking: Some on street

BRASS FLAMINGO

This pretty oasis in downtown Toronto offers lovely and unusual lunches for reasonable prices. The noodle bar, located downstairs from the luxurious Bangkok Garden restaurant, operates on the principle of a salad bar: the base here is noodles, not lettuce, and the toppings are hot meat and vegetables, not cold. Choose rice or egg noodles, then your topping: chicken, pork, shrimp, or fish. The dish costs $5.95. A daily special for the same price may include fried rice, satay, appetizer, and assorted treats.

18 Elm St. (downstairs from the
   Bangkok Garden)
977-6748
Hours: 11:30 A.M. to 4 P.M. Monday to
   Friday, Noon to 4 P.M. Saturday

Closed: Sunday; statutory holidays
Licensed: Full
Payment: Visa, MasterCard, AmEx,
   EnRoute
Parking: Nearby parking lots

LIVING WELL CAFÉ

Known as a good place with late-night hours, this smallish, casual café serves food with a natural bent. Caesar salad is made with a creamy dressing and homemade croutons ($4.25 for a large salad served with rye bread). The vegetarian lasagna, made with zucchini, mushrooms, and green peppers in a tomato sauce, is $5.50. The homemade quiche (a different type every day) is served with salad for $4.95. Stracciatella (Italian chicken-and-egg soup) and tuna or crab melts are not on the menu, but may be ordered. There are thirteen tables inside and more on the patio in summer.

692 Yonge St. (near Isabella St.)
922-6770
Hours: Noon to 4 A.M. Monday to
    Saturday, Noon to 2 A.M. Sunday

Closed: Christmas Eve, New Year's Eve
Licensed: Full
Payment: Visa, MasterCard
Parking: Some on street and side street;
    parking lots nearby

THE BROTHERS

 Peter and Angelo are the Greek brothers who started this place in 1973 and have been running it ever since (one cooks, the other watches and serves). Find your way to one of the green vinyl booths with its arborite table, and settle in for a big feed.

Their chicken sandwiches have long been famous, but they are also known for their peameal bacon sandwiches and their hand-sliced corned beef sandwiches.

The hamburgers are astounding. The meat is thoroughly cooked – old-fashioned style on a grill – and the patty is large enough to double as a wheel on a Volks. It overlaps the bun the way a good schnitzel overlaps the plate: you have to eat your way around the meat on the outside before you get to the bun. And then there's more – the egg burger has a fried egg on top of the meat, and a few fried onion rings are added for good measure. The usual lettuce, tomato, and condiments of your choice top off a culinary skyscraper.

For meals without the bun, you can look to the deli platters, fashioned after those in New York, with several layers of meat like pastrami, corned beef, and so forth. The chips are pretty good; Angelo reports that five percent of his customers order them with mayonnaise. Desserts include homemade toasted coconut-cream pie and creamy rice pudding.

698 Yonge St. (near St. Mary St., in the Church of Scientology Building)
924-5084
Hours: 7:30 A.M. to 8:30 P.M. Monday to Saturday

Closed: Sunday; Christmas Day, New Year's Day
Licensed: Full
Parking: Some on street; parking lot east of Yonge St.

HOP & GRAPE

Prices are fairly low as it is in this homey, well-trodden pub but, if you are a member of any number of groups, you get a further discount. For example, discounts are offered to members of the YMCA and Actor's Equity, and to people who work at CBC, Maclean Hunter, or Women's College Hospital. Also, tourists sometimes get a free dessert if they mention that they saw the restaurant's name in *Teleguide*. Without discounts, steak-and-kidney pie is $5.95, and Scotch eggs served with chutney are $4.95. There's plenty of seating in this two-storey restaurant.

---

14 College St. (near Yonge St.)
923-2715
Hours: 11 A.M. to 1 A.M. Monday to
    Saturday

Closed: Sunday; all major holidays
Licensed: Full
Payment: Visa, MasterCard, AmEx
Parking: Parking lot behind

HUNGARIAN HUT

Watch for good deals in this comfortable restaurant. The early bird special, served between 4 PM and 7 PM, offers soup, salad, main course, dessert, and coffee, for $5.95. The main course changes daily, but you can expect hearty Hungarian fare. Or order just a bowl of chicken soup – it's filled with chicken and vegetables and along with some bread, makes a fine lunch for $3.25. The flaming wooden platter for one will feed two, and features beef or pork tenderloin, wiener schnitzel, chicken, sausage, bacon, and vegetables, for $13.95. Owner Julius Hegebus will do special dinners of "anything you want" for parties of six or more people.

127 Yonge St. (south of Richmond St.)
864-9275
Hours: 11 A.M. to 11 P.M. Monday to Friday, Noon to 11 P.M. Saturday, Sunday

Closed: Sundays in January; Good Friday, Christmas Day, New Year's Day
Licensed: Full
Payment: Visa, AmEx, MasterCard, Diners Club
Parking: Some on street; parking lot on Temperance St.

BAMBOO COURT CHINESE RESTAURANT

Restaurants that serve dim sum are in profusion farther west on Spadina Avenue, but few and far between in this neck of the corporate woods (loosely translated, dim sum means "small eats"). Bamboo Court serves dim sum between 11 A.M. and 2 P.M., and it is fresh and good. Also popular are the shrimp and steamed beef har kau, spring rolls, and barbecued pork bun. Dim sum is served only at lunch. At night the lights go down and the Cantonese platters come out.

103 Yonge St. (near Adelaide St. E.)
363-4391
Hours: 11 A.M. to 11 P.M.

Closed: Never
Licensed: Full
Payment: Visa, MasterCard, AmEx
Parking: Nearby parking lot

KOWLOON DIM SUM RESTAURANT

The Kowloon has long been a favorite for dim sum. It is among the most casual of places, with its arborite tables and tin ashtrays, but the dim sum are prepared to order and come hot and fresh. Dim sum are available all day, and there are over thirty varieties. Among the most favorite are the har kau (four steamed shrimp dumplings for $1.40), and steamed pork dumplings for the same price. Sample the menu and you'll come across lots of little treasures like the soup in pastry and little water-chestnut meatballs. This is a daytime restaurant only.

187 Dundas St. W. (east of University Ave.)
977-3773
Hours: 9 A.M. to 4 P.M. Monday to Friday, 9 A.M. to 5 P.M. Saturday, Sunday
Takeout also

Closed: Christmas
Licensed: No
Payment: Cash only
Parking: Paid parking lots nearby; some on street

THUMPERS

The hamburgers are just great, especially if all the change you have adds up to $2.35. But what's even greater is what they put on them: try garlic or cream cheese under the lettuce and tomato. Or live a little and have their very best burger: cream cheese and smoked oyster. It sounds awful but tastes very good, especially with the potato puffs. Add a real milkshake made with milk and three scoops of ice cream ($1.75) and any one of the superb pies including rhubarb-strawberry or blueberry-banana-cream ($1.75). Thumpers is a very small place with stools for the few who rushed in ahead of you.

99-½ Dundas St. E. (near Church St.)
865-1343
Hours: 11 A.M. to 9 P.M. Monday to
    Friday, 11 A.M. to 6 P.M. Saturday

Closed: Sunday; statutory holidays
Licensed: No
Payment: Cash only
Parking: Street

HART'S

Lots of places serve chicken wings these days, and many of them promise that the wings will be hot. Hart's gives 'em to you mild, medium, and "goodbye guts." They mean it – these wings hurt bad. They're Buffalo-style, which means they're served with a blue cheese dip and vegetables, $3.95 for a small bowl and $6.95 for a large. Also notable is the Caesar salad. There's a deal on it on Wednesdays, when a small salad is served with a bloody Caesar for $5.00. Make a meal of that and the wings, and you'll be on custard for a week. Less daunting is the chicken teriyaki broil, which is broiled chicken in a pita with a pineapple and ginger sauce.

225 Church St. (south of Dundas St. E.)
368-5350
Hours: 11:30 A.M. to 11 P.M. Monday to Thursday, 11:30 A.M. to midnight Friday, 11:30 A.M. to 11 P.M. Saturday

Closed: Sunday; all major holidays
Licensed: Full
Payment: Visa, AmEx, MasterCard
Parking: Street, except between 4 to 6 P.M.

THE SENATOR

This landmark eatery was known as the Busy Bee Diner until 1948, when its name was changed to the Senator. It has undergone changes since then although few were made to the decor, which remains just as you would wish a diner to look – booths, high ceilings, and a long row of stools at a front counter.

Before its most recent incarnation, the Senator was locally loved for its superb egg-salad sandwiches. But now, since Bob Sniderman took the wheel a few years ago, it's loved and lauded for many more things. However, its new popularity has brought crowding and a demand for the management to supply dishes that are more costly than the normal diner fare. A few glasses of the good house wine and a couple of these dishes can result in a hefty bill of the sort you wouldn't expect in a beanery.

But, that said, this is definitely no ordinary diner. The hamburgers – juicy onion, and served with corn relish – are my favorite in all of Toronto. The fries are fabulous, and they taste just the way they should with a strawberry soda make with seltzer the way it should be.

The Senatorte is made from the crust of a whole round loaf of bread. The inside is taken out and replaced with ham, salami, provolone cheese, peppers, and other vegetables, like the best and prettiest Dagwood sandwich you ever made ($5.95 for a quarter). The crab cakes are little fat wheels of fish, crab, cream, and onions ($7.95 for two cakes). If any Cajun-creole specialities are available, try them. And if you can get there for the enormous breakfast, do – but do it when you can go back to sleep afterwards.

249 Victoria St. (south of Dundas St.
E.)
364-7517
Hours: 8 A.M. to 11 P.M. Tuesday to
Friday, 9 A.M. to 11 P.M. Saturday,
8 A.M. to 5 P.M. Monday

Closed: Sunday; and all major holidays
Licensed: Full
Payment: Visa, MasterCard
Parking: Some on street; parking lot
nearby

BERSANI & CARLEVALE

This is a chic place, but the prices are good and the food can be excellent. Especially recommended here are the pizzas, particularly those with brie and other special toppings such as olives, leeks, and eggplant. The crusts are thin and the toppings wonderfully combined.

595 Bay St. (in the Atrium on Bay)
595-0881
Hours: 8 A.M. to midnight Monday to
    Saturday

Closed: Sunday; all statutory holidays.
Licensed: Full
Payment: Visa
Parking: Paid underground; on street
    after business hours

W.D. KONES

Some of the flavors are a mite too sweet (the pralines 'n' cream, for instance), but the chocolate chocolate chip is like eating a cold, wet, wonderful chocolate bar. The cones are huge — a sort of crispy waffle shaped into a cone — and they're filled to the ceiling with huge scoops of ice cream. One recent cone lasted the whole car ride from the downtown store to Bathurst and St. Clair. The banana split is the old fashioned kind, made up of three different flavors of ice cream, chocolate sauce, nuts, fruit, and whipped cream. It makes a good dinner for $5.95. You can create your own sundae with two scoops of any flavor of ice cream plus a topping for $2.75, or four scoops for $3.50. Twenty-three ounce milkshakes cost $2.50.

(in the Atrium on Bay at Edward St.)
585-2269
Hours: Summer: 10 A.M. to midnight Monday to Saturday, Noon to 10 P.M. Sunday. Winter: 10 A.M. to 10 P.M. Monday to Saturday, Noon to 8 P.M. Sunday

Closed: Christmas Day, Thanksgiving, Easter
Licensed: No
Payment: Cash only
Parking: Some on street; underground in the Atrium

WOK & BOWL

Toronto now has several of these wok restaurants, and they're lots of fun. Cheap too, if you know how to do it. The principle is that noodles are the base and the toppings are what cost. If you order a bowl of noodles with stir-fried vegetables or just chicken, your meal will be cheaper than if you order a bowl of noodles and ask them to put seafood on top. The Wok & Bowl opened in August of 1985. The restaurant takes its name from its most popular dish, which is a bowl of deep-fried noodles topped with scallops and chicken ($8.99). Note the late closing hours on the weekend.

195 Dundas St. W. (west of University Ave.)
591-8833
Hours: 11 A.M. to 11 P.M. Monday to Thursday, 11 A.M. to 4 A.M. Friday, Saturday, 4 P.M. to 10 P.M. Sunday
Takeout also

Closed: For lunch on public holidays, but open for dinner
Licensed: Full
Payment: Visa, MasterCard, AmEx
Parking: Paid lots nearby; some on street

YING KING COURT RESTAURANT

The ingredients here are as fresh as they come, and prices are good. Dim sum are served every day for lunch and have an edge on many others on the block because of the freshness and variety. In the evenings, the food is quite classically Cantonese. Chopped meats and vegetables are served rolled in lettuce for $6.55. Vegetables and seafoods are stir fried and priced according to ingredients. Ying King is a fairly large (250-seat) restaurant, comfortably decorated but not overdone. Owner Winnie Zee asks that readers be reminded that this is no ordinary chop suey joint.

123–A Dundas St. W. (second floor) (west of Bay St.)
977-8828
Hours: 10 A.M. to midnight seven days
Takeout also

Closed: Never (not even Chinese New Year)
Licensed: Full
Payment: Visa, MasterCard, AmEx
Parking: Paid lots nearby; some on street

ABUNDANCE

Abundance must be included for its excellent hamburgers. The plain burger is fine, but even finer is the burger with herb-garlic cheese and sautéed mushrooms ($6.50), or the burger with Swiss cheese and sautéed onions (also $6.50). Fries are homemade and they taste it. The carrot cake once won an award as the best in the city. One of the owners is with the National Ballet, hence the pun on "dance".

81 Church St. (at Adelaide St. E.)
368-2867
Hours: 11 A.M. to 1 A.M. Monday to
    Saturday

Closed: Sunday; Christmas Day
Licensed: Full
Payment: Visa, MasterCard, AmEx
Parking: Street; nearby parking lot

EMILIO'S

Emilio's takeout counter is a good bet for lunches. The sandwiches are a bit pricey, but very good and very inventive. The soups are too, especially the gazpacho, the potato-cheddar-chili, and cream of cauliflower (about $3.00).

127 Queen St. E. (near Jarvis St.)
366-3354
Hours for takeout counter: 11:30 A.M.to
    4 P.M. Monday to Saturday

Closed: Sunday; all major holidays
Licensed: No
Payment: Visa, MasterCard, AmEx
Parking: street; parking lot across the
    street

JOE ALLEN

This is the Toronto branch of the Joe Allen group (others are in New York, Los Angeles, London, and Paris), a classy place with its understated entrance and spiffy clientele, many with theatrical associations. It has a large menu with many entrées priced outside of our range, but within it are the superb hamburgers that come thick, juicy, and generously topped with many flavor variations. The fries are very good, and can be ordered to the color you like – from pale to very dark (darker is crunchier). Don't miss the sweet potato fries ($1.75), and if you like salads, there are big ones and plenty of choice ($5.75 to $6.50). The bar is unusually well stocked, so there is a variety of imported beer to accompany your hamburger and fries, as well as many off-beat labels. Joe Allen tries for class in every direction, and promises no silly drinks with umbrellas.

86 John St. (off Adelaide St. W., two blocks east of Spadina Ave.)
593-9404
Hours: 11:30 A.M. to 1 A.M. Monday to Saturday, 11:30 A.M. to midnight Sunday

Closed: Christmas Day
Licensed: Full
Payment: Visa, AmEx, Diners Club
Parking: Street; parking lot next door

WHEAT SHEAF TAVERN

A longstanding favorite hangout of sports folk, this is not your regular sort of dive: it's an historic one, since it first opened in 1849. The Wheat Sheaf is particularly packed and happy during the Toronto Blue Jays season. The chicken wings are terrific (ten wings for $2.50); the Louisville Slugger is a ten-ounce hot dog for $1.95. Owner Jerry Borne, who has run for Toronto alderman in the past, can often be found eating down the block at Barney's on Queen St. W. but that doesn't mean his own food isn't good.

667 King St. W. (at Bathurst St.)
364-3996
Hours: 11 A.M. to 1 A.M. Monday to
    Saturday

Closed: Sunday
Licensed: Full
Payment: Visa
Parking: Street

THE WHISTLING OYSTER

Downstairs from the Filet of Sole Restaurant (a frantically popular, casual seafood restaurant) is the Whistling Oyster, essentially a bar with a few banquettes, tables, and stools. There you can have escargotti Alfredo for $3.99 or a number of other such specials which, like the escargot, are Italian in theme and feature seafood. There are fresh oysters, of course, and many other fish and shellfish dishes.

11 Duncan St. (downstairs) (north off
   King St. W., west of University Ave.)
598-7707
Hours: 11:30 A.M. to 1 A.M. Monday to
   Saturday, Noon to 10 P.M. Sunday

Closed: Christmas Day
Licences: Full
Payment: Visa, MasterCard, AmEx
Parking: Street, side streets; some
   parking lots nearby

MOVENPICK RESTAURANTS OF SWITZERLAND

A very large restaurant (380 seats), part of a chain based in Switzerland, the Movenpick is very popular with the local business lunchers, who like the good food and moderate prices. Especially recommended is the Swiss Farmer's Lunch for Sunday brunch, from 11 A.M. to 3 P.M.. The price, $17.95, might seem a bit high, but is well worth it for the enormous array of wonderful meats, fish, cheeses, and baked goods. Take it slow, a course at a time, and you can spend some very happy hours here.

165 York St. (south of Richmond St.)
366-5234
Hours: 7 A.M. to midnight Monday to
   Saturday, 7 A.M. to 11 P.M. Sunday,
   11 A.M. to 3 P.M. Sunday brunch

Closed: At 10 P.M. on Christmas Day
Licensed: Full
Payment: Visa, MasterCard, AmEx
Parking: Under building

CABBAGETOWN

The mixture of restaurants and taverns in Cabbagetown is as varied as the population and the houses they live in — some are just as they were thirty years ago, others are a reflection of the eager renovators that have brightened the houses and gladdened the hearts of local proprietors. This is an area to explore, poking through grocery stores on the way. In the summer, get an ice cream cone and wander through the local zoo. In any season, drop in on the caterers Daniel et Daniel on Carlton Street and see what's in the showcases. Everything's tempting, but be sure to take home some chocolate mousse cake.

On Parliament Street, try Sombreros' tacos or a souffle at Le Souffle, or go sit at the bar and look at the astounding paintings and windows at Le Canard Enchaine on Amelia Street. The metamorphosis of Cabbagetown has been as dramatic in food as it has in architecture.

CAP'S BAR & GRILL

The double phone numbers for this bar-restaurant give the first clue: this is a busy spot. It draws locals and others who may have come from Maple Leaf Gardens or fresh from other events to chat about the latest football or hockey scores. If you've ever watched the "man in the pub" TV commentaries after sports events, chances are the pub was Cap's. The neon chicken in the window tells you what to order.

Chicken wings are free with drinks from 5 P.M. to 7 P.M. most nights. They're fine, fairly hot, if you want — and who can argue with the price? The rest of the time they're $4.95 for a basket of ten wings. Other things to order include chicken fingers and a garlicky-good Caesar salad. This is a very cheery place, with special events almost daily that boost the already friendly fracas. Monday is games night; Tuesday is Wing Ding night, when you get two orders of wings for the price of one; and Wednesday is Mexican night, when sangria and tacos are 99 cents each. Finger snacks are complimentary from 5 P.M. to 7 P.M. Monday to Saturday.

---

572 Jarvis St. (near Charles St. E.)
924-8555 (if busy, call 925-8504)
Hours: 11 A.M. to 1 A.M. Monday to
    Saturday, Noon to 11 P.M. Sunday

Closed: Christmas Day, Boxing Day
Licensed: Full
Payment: Visa, MasterCard, AmEx
Parking: Street

TIMOTHY'S CHICKEN

Timothy's has been named in some surveys as having the best tandoori chicken in town. It hasn't but it's still good, especially for Cabbagetown, a neighborhood not known for its Indian restaurants. Another point in its favor is that the tandoori can be prepared for takeout or delivery. Wherever you eat it, have it the traditional way, with naan (Indian bread). Tandoori chicken costs $5.05 for a quarter of a chicken if you eat it in; $4.55 if you take it out. You also can limit your tandoori to just wings. Timothy's barbecued chicken also is very popular ($4.25 to eat in; $3.75 to take out). If you are eating in, try the mulligatawny soup; it's spicy and delicious. The restaurant is small and comfortable.

556 Parliament St. (near Wellesley St.)
964-7583
Hours: 11:30 A.M. to 11 P.M. Monday
   to Thursday, 11:30 A.M. to midnight
   Friday, Saturday, 4 P.M. to 10:30
   P.M. Sunday
Takeout and delivery also

Closed: Christmas Day, Boxing Day
Licensed: Beer and wine
Payment: Visa, MasterCard
Parking: Street

THE PEASANT'S LARDER

One of the owners describes this casual, frolicky restaurant as having "home-cooked, real, esoteric Mexican food and the greatest Margaritas in town." And if you don't like it, it's probably your own fault. For instance, you're in charge of your own tacos. You cook them yourself at the table and then assemble them from a platter of meats, cheeses, and sauces — a lot like those birthday parties where you build your own sundae, or salad bars where you build your own salad, using more chickpeas and less iceberg lettuce than the cost-efficient restaurant might have chosen for you. The combination platter of enchilada, burrito, taco, refried beans, and rice is called "Nag Nag Nag"; it costs $9.95, a stiff price, but is a generous plateful.

This is a very cheerful place where they seem aggravated if you're not having as much fun as they are. Take the kids.

---

221 Carlton St. (west of Parliament St.)
967-9141
Hours: Noon to 10 P.M. Tuesday to
    Thursday, Noon to 11 P.M. Friday,
    Saturday, 5 P.M. to 10 P.M. Sunday

Closed: Monday
Licensed: Full
Payment: Visa, AmEx, MasterCard
Parking: Street

BRASSERIE LES ARTISTES

This casual, European-style café is run by two maitre d's who were formerly at the Windsor Arms restaurants, and it specializes in good, lightly creative bistro food that's pretty reasonably priced. With its small marble tables, soft lighting, and wall posters, it's the kind of place where you'd expect to see writers in corners by themselves. There are some booths and more tables. On the blackboard menu (brought to your table on an easel) you may find steak and frites, or grilled liver. There's always some fresh seafood, the best of which is the moules marinière. Chicken and beef are always available, but what I like best are the specials that are often hard to find elsewhere, like grilled calves liver served with herb butter ($7.95), and the special sausages. The sausages are made on the premises and are terrific. There may be bratwurst, or a spicy pepper toulouse, or merguez from Algeria. The andouillette (sausages encased in tripe and entrails) sound so forbidding that they must be good — and they are.

243 Carlton St. (just west of Parliament St.)
963-9433
Hours: 11:30 A.M. to 2:30 P.M.; 5:30 P.M. to 10 P.M. Monday to Wednesday, 11:30 A.M. to 2:30 P.M.; 5:30 P.M. to 11 P.M. Thursday to Saturday

Closed: Sunday; statutory holidays
Licensed: Full
Payment: Visa, AmEx, MasterCard
Parking: Street

THE DANFORTH

Bloor Street runs nearly the entire width of Toronto, and is a travelogue of ethnicity every mile of the way. The section we call "the Danforth," stretching east from Broadview Avenue, is mainly Greek — with street signs to prove it. It had been said that more shishkebobs are sold along the Danforth than have been consumed in Corfu. The larger restaurants have open kitchens where you can select your meal from steam tables. The Danforth also is the home of the best and brightest produce stores like Sunkist and Greenview, open at all hours. Don't miss the Pallas Bakery's almond trumans, which are almond paste encased in dark, bittersweet chocolate; or their two-storey almond cookies. Especially on summer evenings, the streets are very busy with both vehicular and pedestrian traffic. Watch for summer street festivals with their wagonfuls of good food.

The strip on Gerrard, south of Danforth between Broadview and Coxwell, is beginning to be a treasure trove of excellent and inexpensive Chinese restaurants. The Saigon houses a series of kiosks where you can collect various dishes. Eat them at the tables provided or take them home. Don't miss the noodle dishes at Tasty Counter.

NEWFOUNDLANDER TAVERN & STEAK HOUSE

This is a foot-stomping, back-slapping sort of place — home away from home for the Atlantic Canadians for whom life has less meaning without cod. Cod is there in happy profusion in the fish n' brewis, which combines salt cod with moistened hardtack, crispy fried salt pork (scrunchions), and onions. If you grew up with it, it's a treat ($3.50). Cod tongues are pan fried with salt pork and served with boiled potatoes ($5.50), and fish cakes made with mashed potatoes are $3.50. There's down-east music on the juke box and a down-east live band on the weekends. Owner Chris Issariotis boasts that he sold the first beer to the American Sixth Fleet in Greece in 1940.

185 Danforth Ave. (near Broadview Ave.)
469-1916
Hours: 11 A.M. to 1 A.M. Monday to Saturday, 11:30 A.M. to 11 P.M. Sunday

Closed: Christmas Day, New Year's Day
Licensed: Full
Payment: Visa, MasterCard, AmEx
Parking: Street; parking lot across street

THE WILLOW RESTAURANT

The name suggests cucumber sandwiches and cream soups, but the Willow is actually a Mexican-style restaurant, quite different from the large number of Greek restaurants in the area. Its increasing popularity is partly due to the cheerful service and the generally congenial and casual atmosphere.

Try two of the cheesey appetizers: the Mexican Mice, five jalapeño peppers stuffed with Monterey Jack cheese and deep fried (called "Mice" because the stems of the peppers look like mice tails), and Cheese in a Carriage, which is Monterey Jack again, breaded and deep fried crusty outside and runny inside. It's served with a spicy salsa for dipping. Try the soups, too, the bean soup especially ($1.95). Entrées include an enchilada plate, which is like an enchilada torte, stacked with different fillings and topped with cheese, a good deal at $7.95 because two can split it.

For those who wish more prosaic fare, there are hamburgers and grilled seafood. The brunch menu on Saturday and Sunday offers spicy variations on eggs, including huevos rancheros for $4.50. There also are some deals on drinks: Monday, sangria is $1.49 for a seven-ounce glass; Tuesday, a seven-ounce glass of wine is also $1.49.

---

193 Danforth Ave. (at Broadview)
469-5315
Hours: 11:30 A.M. to midnight Monday
    to Saturday, 11 A.M. to 10 P.M.
    Sunday

Closed: Christmas Day and Boxing Day
Licensed: Full
Payment: Visa, MasterCard, AmEx
Parking: Street

QUINN'S TAVERN

The chicken wings are the food specialty here, although other distractions include the bar, dance floor, and dart board. The sauce is homemade and is offered from mild to hot. Hot is *really* hot. The regular price is $3.75 for ten, but they are half-price on Tuesday nights. They aren't the cheapest in town, as they once were (the cheapest I've seen so far are 5 cents apiece — cheaper than you can get them raw at the supermarket), but Quinn's wings taste great.

323 Danforth Rd. (at Birchmount)
694-2031
Hours: 11 A.M. to 1 A.M. Monday to
    Saturday, 11 A.M. to 11 P.M.
    Sunday

Closed: Christmas Day
Licensed: Full
Payment: Visa, AmEx, MasterCard
Parking: Street; parking lot at back

SHER-E-PUNJAB

One of Toronto's most popular Indian restaurants, the Sher-E-Punjab has been on the Danforth for thirteen years. The restaurant now seats eighty. The atmosphere has remained casual and the food reliable. Order the vegetable pakoras ($2 for six pieces) and the tandoori chicken ($2) as appetizers, and then try the chicken jalfreze, goat or pork curry. If you tell them you want it hot, they'll believe you. It's a family owned and run restaurant — all the cooking is done by mom and daughter, while dad tells you what's good and then serves it.

Sher-E-Punjab becomes frantically busy on weekend nights between 7 p.m. and 9 p.m., so leisurely dining might best be accomplished at other times.

351 Danforth Avenue
465-2125
Hours: 4 P.M. to 11 P.M. Monday to
 Saturday, 4 P.M. to 10 P.M. Sunday
Takeout also

Closed: Christmas Eve, New Year's Day
Licensed: Full
Payment: Visa, MasterCard, AmEx,
 Diner's Club
Parking: Street

ASTORIA SHISH KEBOB RESTAURANT

Although the Astoria has been there for about fifteen years (and claims to be the first souvlaki place on the Danforth), it caught on only a few years ago, so at prime time (almost any evening) there is usually a wait. The word has spread about their having the best souvlaki sandwiches and the best prices.

The Astoria souvlaki sandwiches, which are terrific, are made with a long skewer of grilled lamb cubes, a few pieces of onion, and a few slices of tomato, laid on a long sesame seed bun which is given a fast toasting on the grill. The bun is painted with what the menu calls a "special garlic sauce," which old timers know as tzadziki — a mixture of dense yogurt with lots of fresh garlic. It spreads like cream cheese, but has a flavor rich and satisfying enough to disguise the fact that it's made up of two perfectly nutritious ingredients. It wouldn't be going too far to say that it's the tzadziki that elevates this sandwich from what would otherwise be some grilled lamb on a bun. Order extra.

The stars of the menu are the meats that are cooked on the long grill that's in the window, and that includes the tiny quail (served as an appetizer with fresh lemon), lamb chops, pork chops, and hamburgers. The dinner plates, which may be based on lamb or beef, will also include rice, roasted Greek potatoes, and Greek salad, for $6.95 — a whacking great meal that would feed two. The Greek salad isn't bad, if you don't mind its heavy reliance on iceberg lettuce, and that the only thing it has in common with the genuine article is feta cheese and olives.

This is a casual restaurant that is very noisy on weekends. It's usually worthwhile to wait for a table because turnover is fast. The waiter won't write anything down, no matter how many there are at your table, and always gets the order right.

400 Danforth Ave. (near Chester Ave.)
463-2838
Hours: 11 A.M. to 1 A.M. seven days

Closed: Easter, Christmas Eve and Day
Licensed: Full
Payment: Visa, AmEx
Parking: Street; parking lot at back

OMONIA SHISKABOB RESTAURANT

Like many of the other shishkebob restaurants along the Danforth, the Omonia has the grill in the front window and the essential menu items like the shishkebob sandwich ($2.95) and generous platters of various grilled meats, Greek potatoes, and rice tzadziki. The menu is more extensive than at some of the other shishkebob houses, and the interior of the Omonia is slightly more refined, although it's hardly posh. In the summer, there are tables on a platform outside the side entrance.

Although there are those who will sneer at any departure from the simple grilled meats that make places like the Omonia so good, you might try the gyros, better here than at many other places. These are sandwiches, not unlike donairs. The meat is a highly seasoned, compressed meat of lamb and beef, which is roasted on a vertical spit and then shaved off. The meat is laid flat on an unopened pita bun, which has been oiled and toasted on the grill. On top of the meat is laid raw onion, tomato, feta cheese, and tzadziki. The pita is then rolled around the filling and presented to you in a cone. It is a messy, delicious meal, which far surpasses a hamburger for flavor and satisfying mouth-feel. There are other specialities, including the barbecued lamb and the pork sausages, made big and spicy on the premises. These specialities are served on platters with potatoes and vegetables for $6.95 and $6.60, respectively.

The Omonia's tzadziki is very rich and full of garlic. You might consider taking home a carton — it's very good with cheese pirogies. The shishkebob sandwich is also good for take-out.

426 Danforth Ave.

465-2129

Hours: 11 A.M. to 1 A.M. Monday to
Friday, 11 A.M. to 3 A.M. Saturday,
Sunday

Takeout also

Closed: Never

Licensed: Full

Payment: Visa, AmEx

Parking: Street; parking lot at the back

ODYSSEY RESTAURANT & DINING LOUNGE

This large and comfortable dining room serves the heartiest of Greek food. The calamari, pita, and huge Greek salads are recommended. Other popular meals include the moussaka made with ground beef, rather than the traditional lamb, served with potatoes, overdone green beans, and rice ($7.00 at dinner, less at lunch). A plateful of roast lamb and accompaniments costs $7.00. The Odyssey has been overstuffing its clients for more than twenty years.

477 Danforth Ave. (near Logan Ave.)
465-2451
Hours: 11 A.M. to 1 A.M. Sunday to
    Thursday, 11 A.M. to 2 A.M. Friday,
    Saturday

Closed: Never
Licensed: Full
Payment: Visa, MasterCard, AmEx
Parking: Street

PARTNER'S RESTAURANT INC.

Partner's was first recommended for its potato skins, which are very good, especially if they're followed by a hamburger. The burgers may be made from beef, lamb, veal, or chicken (who said hamburgers *had* to made from beef?) What you add to the meat patty depends on what you think belongs with it. The club burger, for $6.50, is modeled on the club sandwich and has everything you'd look for in its namesake, plus a few odd extras: peameal bacon, apples, tomatoes, and mayo. The cordon bleu burger ($6.75) is stuffed with prosciutto and Swiss cheese. These are big hamburgers, with a price to match. The basic burger costs $4.50, and added items are 40 cents each.

The menu has expanded greatly since the first Partner's opened five years ago. There now are pastas, vegetarian plates, a fresh fruit plate, and more appetizers. It is very much a neighborhood restaurant, with items like the honey-garlic ribs, which aren't on the menu but are ordered by the regulars.

---

836 Danforth Ave. (at Jones Ave.)
469-1539
(Other locations: 4985 Yonge St. and
   765 Mount Pleasant Rd.)
Hours: 11:30 A.M. to 1 A.M. (kitchen
   closes at midnight) Monday to
   Friday, 4 P.M. to 1 A.M. Saturday,
   Sunday

Closed: All statutory holidays
Licensed: Full
Payment: Visa, AmEx
Parking: Street; nearby parking lots

SHALA-MAR DINING ROOM

Those who once loved the Indian food at the Koh-I-Noor at Bay and Davenport happily followed the restaurant to its new name and location four years ago. The food is Indian and Pakistani, with the emphasis on meat dishes. The meat curries cost about $5.00. Have the samosas and pakora to help round out the meal.

427 Donlands Ave. (near O'Connor Dr.)
425-3663
Hours: Noon to 10 P.M. Tuesday to
    Thursday, Noon to midnight Friday,
    Saturday, Sunday

Closed: Monday
Licensed: Full
Payment: Visa, MasterCard, AmEx
Parking: Street; parking lot at rear

EATING COUNTER II

This eating counter is a joint venture with the restaurant of the same name that's located at 41 Baldwin Street. Opened in 1984, it promises to be as popular and as good. Recommended are hot-and-sour soup ($2.15, serves two), fried pork with special sauce on a sizzling hot plate ($6.25), and chicken with black bean sauce on a sizzling hot plate ($5.25). It is a fairly large restaurant, with twenty-five tables.

2183 Danforth Ave. (east of Woodbine Ave.)
690-5666
Hours: 11 A.M. to 11 P.M. seven days
Takeout also

Closed: Statutory holidays
Licensed: No
Payment: Cash only
Parking: At rear, on street

GERRARD STREET EAST

The patchwork of taverns and pizza places that is Queen Street East abruptly gives way to a fascinating microcosm of a street in an Indian city, where store windows show saris and silver jewellry. Mostly East Indian, the shops and restaurants are lively with colorful products and the people who buy them.

Sunday is the day to stroll the area around Gerrard Street and Coxwell Avenue. Stop at the Milan Department Store for the big, delicious samosas offered in a bin out front for 50 cents each. The samosas arrive at 1 P.M. and, once they're gone, that's it for the day. Try the Chaat Hut for Indian appetizers of small wafers sprinkled with cumin and topped with mango chutney and yogurt. African restaurants also are beginning to appear in this neighborhood. Generally the restaurants in this area are very casual, inexpensive, and often very good.

CHILES MEXICAN FLAVORS

Elisabeth Escobar and Desmond Poons opened Chiles four years ago, and for the few months before they were discovered served burritos, tacos, and wonderful mixed fruit drinks to an audience starved for the quality Mexican food they offered. Then they were discovered: the tiny and very pretty shop was inundated, but somehow they handled it, increasing their speed and their menu. Now it's not always as busy as it was in those frenetic days, and sometimes not as good as it was before then, but the colorful place is still good fun. The menu has expanded in some ways, contracted in others, but I still like the burritos, fat and full of meat, chicken, or vegetables, and the taquitos (tiny corn tortillas) come four to an order — one stuffed with Monterey Jack cheese, another with chicken and coriander, all of them served with a spicy salsa and refried beans. The black bean soup also is very popular. There are some full-meal specials like swordfish steak and that baffling Mexican dish pollo en mole, which is chicken in a chocolate sauce. The dish isn't as bizarre as it sounds, but I prefer the hand-held foods.

The fruit drinks are a big feature. Beware of the coconut-based drinks if you're having a meal, because they are very filling — save them for thirsty summer days. With the meals, have other drinks like the pineapple or banana coolers.

This is a colorful and cheering place for a quick meal.

---

936 Gerrard St. E. (near Pape Ave.)
469-1247
Hours: 4 P.M. to 11 P.M. seven days
Takeout and delivery also

Closed: Most statutory holidays,
    January 6 (Ethiopian Christmas)
Licensed: Full
Payment: Visa, MasterCard, AmEx
Parking: Street

MOTI MAHAL RESTAURANT

This is one of the best places in Toronto for Indian food, and it's also about the least expensive. To get both of those qualities in the same place, something's got to go — and what goes here is the decor. There are only a few tables and those are arborite with odd tin ashtrays on them. That's because the Moti Mahal is designed for takeout, and the tables are best for waiting at while your order is being made up. Go to the back and choose what you want from the large containers: bryani, gosht, or goat curry. Make a meal of tandoori chicken ($8.00 for a full chicken) and have some naan to go with it, or order goat saag with spinach ($3.50). Try the malai kofta vegetable balls for $2.25. Tell them how many chapatis or paraunthas you want or, if you prefer, rice to balance the spiciness. It all comes with some mint sauce or any of the usual condiments, like raita or dal, that you'd expect. The foods are served in styrofoam containers so you can take them home or carry them on a tray to a table. There is a counter of desserts, including those very sweet colored bars if you like them. Don't miss the excellent spicy pepper cashews ($7.00 per pound). Order them to eat while you're waiting for your order to be ready. The last time I was there, two of us ate our heads off for $16, including cashews.

1422 Gerrard St. E. (near Coxwell
Ave.)
461-3111
Hours: 11:30 A.M. to 11 P.M. Friday,
Saturday, Sunday, 11:30 A.M. to
10:30 P.M. Monday, Wednesday,
Thursday
Takeout mainly

Closed: Tuesday in the winter
Licensed: No
Payment: Visa, MasterCard
Parking: Street

KAMEL CHAT

This is a terrifically entertaining place to stop off after dinner in any of the Indian restaurants in this area. Ask for the item called pan, which is made from betel leaves and betel nuts, and is popular throughout Asia (you might remember it as the favorite chew of the character Bloody Mary in "South Pacific"). For 40 cents, the pleasant man behind the counter will paint a betel leaf (which is about the size of a large oak leaf,) with layers of sweet spices and some silver leaf, common to Indian cooking. He tops this with coconut and preserved rose leaves, and rolls it up to the size of a small dumpling. Put the whole thing in your mouth and chew. In a few seconds, your mouth will be full of juices. You can form the contents of your mouth into a ball and spit it out, or you can chew it up and swallow it. It tastes a bit odd if you aren't used to that sort of thing, but it's all good, clean fun, and it's said to be wonderful for digestion.

1427 Gerrard St. E. (near Coxwell Ave.)
Hours: 11 A.M. to 10 P.M. Friday to Sunday
Takeout only

Closed: Monday to Thursday
Licensed: No
Payment: Cash only
Parking: Street

SHAI DABAR

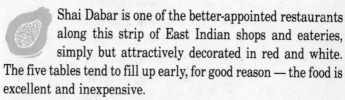 Shai Dabar is one of the better-appointed restaurants along this strip of East Indian shops and eateries, simply but attractively decorated in red and white. The five tables tend to fill up early, for good reason — the food is excellent and inexpensive.

To start, order the meat samosas, which are triangular-shaped deep-fried pastries filled with meat or vegetables. The meat ones are the best. Order too the vegetable pakhoras, little deep-fried jumbles of spinach and onion. Both are eaten with the fingers and both are served with a sweet-sour sauce of tomato, lemon, carrots, and onion. The menu on the wall isn't large and, so far, each dish has been very good. Chicken jalfrezi ($5.95) is chicken that has been twice cooked: first the meat is barbecued, then it is simmered with tomatoes and green peppers and flavored with lime, coriander, and chilies. The goat gosht (goat meat cooked with yogurt and spices) is superb. The corma dishes, also flavored with yogurt are excellent (chicken: $3.75, mutton: $3.95).

Vegetable thali looks like a TV dinner. Served on a stainless steel tray that is divided into sections, thali is a selection of vegetable concoctions, served with rice, chapati, and papadums. Some Indian restaurants offer this as a meal for one; it makes a very good lunch.

All of the meals are served with sauces that add flavor and also cool the food, such as a simple dal lentil sauce, crushed coriander and lime juice, and crushed pomegranate mixed with yogurt. A very full meal, including soft drinks, lassi (a yogurt drink), or a mango milkshake, will cost about $10 per person.

1435 Gerrard St. E. (near Coxwell
   Ave.)
463-4354
Hours: Noon to 9:30 P.M. Monday,
   Tuesday, Noon to 10 P.M. Thursday,
   5 P.M. to 10:30 P.M. Friday, Noon to
   10 P.M. Saturday, Sunday
Takeout available

Closed: Wednesday
Payment: Visa
Parking: Street

THE BEACH

This is an attractive community with a distinctive and cohesive feeling that is apparent in many of the restaurants. There are a lot of restaurants now — so many, in fact, that legislation has been demanded to limit future ones.

Within two city blocks there's a choice of everything from hot dogs to high chic. Generally, though, the area is casual, and the best of the food is informal. The emphasis is on natural foods, and although there are lots of fast foods, everyone insists they are made with only natural ingredients.

By extending the area reviewed to Kingston Road (hopeful realtors have extended the boundaries much farther), several pubs have been included. Most support the current fad for chicken wings yet still offer the fare of their British mentors, which means you are likely to encounter shepherd's pie and the like. A few of the old lunch counters cling to life, so there are places for inexpensive breakfasts. Among these is the Garden Gate Restaurant, locally known as "the GOOF" since some of the letters in the "good food" sign faded. For something a little more upscale, try the Toriichi, a wonderful Japanese-French restaurant at Queen and Greenwood.

Although many people enjoy just driving along Queen Street, this is a street that is made for walking, talking and eating ice cream in the summer and fish and chips year-round. The Nova Fish Store was one of the area's earliest restaurants, and is still considered to have the best fish and chips in the neighborhood.

LICK'S BURGER & ICE CREAM SHOPS

Lick's initial fame was due to its ice cream, but this popular restaurant has gone on to glory because of its hamburgers, or "homeburgers" as Lick's prefers to call them. The homey burgers are made of six ounce patties of fresh, lean ground beef, served on fresh buns with an vast variety of toppings. The basic burger is $2.35, the burger you build is $2.65. The chili, though not perfect, is better than most. Milkshakes are made with any of the available sixteen flavors of ice cream, and are worth mentioning because too many others come processed, in a mushy squirt, with indistinguishable origins. Ice cream also is served in sundaes ($2.65) with a variety of toppings including fresh fruit.

Although there are counters at which you can perch and tables upstairs, this is not a place for relaxed dining, especially when the rush is on. When the weather's nice, take your goodies to the park down the street, where there are benches and small tables.

1960 Queen St. E. (east of Woodbine Ave.)
Two other locations: 2383 Kingston Rd., and 2245 Yonge St.
691-2305
Hours: 11 A.M. to 11 P.M. seven days
Takeout also

Closed: Christmas Day
Licensed: No
Payment: Cash only
Parking: Some on street

JONATHAN'S HAMBURGERS

To survive directly across the street from Lick's stronghold, something here has to be good. Lots of things are, including burgers, thick and juicy ($2.25, extra for toppings); and wings, hot or honey-garlic (nine for $2.95). The homemade fries and homemade potato chips are terrific. There is some seating on stools.

1961 Queen St. E. (near Kenilworth Ave.)
691-6888
Hours: 11 A.M. to 2 A.M. Monday to Thursday, 11 A.M. to 3 A.M. Friday, Saturday, 11 A.M. to 1 A.M. Sunday
Takeout also

Closed: Phone and check on holidays
Licensed: No
Payment: Cash only
Parking: Street

SUNSET GRILL

This addition to the Beach area became quickly known by local bargain-seekers for its inexpensive all-day breakfasts – three eggs, homefries, peameal bacon or sausage and nice, thick toast cost $3.75. Burgers are $2.25, $2.50 with Swiss or cheddar cheese. There are twelve tables and a counter with four stools. The owners drive down daily from north of Agincourt to open at 7 AM.

2006 Queen St. E. (near Bellefair Ave.)
690-9985
Hours: 7 A.M. to 8 P.M. seven days

Closed: Christmas Day, maybe
Licensed: No
Payment: Cash only
Parking: Street

NOVA FISH STORE

The Nova is considered to have the area's best fish and chips, an opinion evidenced by the waiting line-ups in the summer. The fish is fresh and the batter crusty and sweet, cooked with good grease. It is a small restaurant with only six tables, so takeout is suggested.

2209 Queen St. E. (near Leuty Ave.)
699-1885
Hours: 11 A.M. to 7 P.M. Tuesday,
    Wednesday, Thursday, Saturday, 11
    A.M. to 8 P.M. Friday
Takeout also

Closed: Sunday, Monday; some
    holidays
Licensed: No
Payment: Cash only
Parking: Street

FITZGERALD'S RESTAURANT

A popular spot, this old pub has been in the area for about seven years. Chicken-wing lovers should be warned that the ones served here are the hottest in town — beyond the capacity of even the most seasoned palate. Avoid those and ask for what they think are the medium-hot wings. The wings are on special on Wednesday nights for 15 cents each. Hamburgers, also called Fitzburgers, are $3.25. One of those and the competent Caesar salad are good alternatives.

2298 Queen St. E. (near Scarborough Rd.)
691-1393
Hours: Noon to 1 A.M. Monday to Saturday, 11 A.M. to 11 P.M. Sunday

Closed: Statutory holidays
Licensed: Full
Payment: Visa, MasterCard
Parking: Street

BOARDWALK CAFÉ

The Boardwalk Café is the place to find good Italian food at fair prices. The veal Parmesan dinner, served with salad and bread, is $6.75; the lasagna dinner is $5.95, while a generous portion of gnocchi with bread is $4.95. Owner Mario Dipoce does all the preparation and cooking, and thinks it isn't fair that people miss his restaurant just because it's two doors off the beaten track of Queen Street. He's right.

2 Wheeler Ave. (just north of Queen
   St. E.)
694-4795
Hours: Winter: Noon to 10:30 P.M.
   seven days, Summer: Noon to
   midnight seven days
Takeout also

Closed: Christmas Day, New Year's Day
Licensed: No
Payment: Visa, MasterCard
Parking: Street

THE GROVER EXCHANGE

 So named because the location once was a telephone exchange, the Grover Exchange is a sister restaurant to the Hargrave Exchange at 1106 Danforth Avenue. It is a comfortable and popular local pub. There are specials like steak and kidney pie and shepherd's pie for the old-fashioned pub flavor, and others, like the Buffalo-style chicken wings, that remind you it's a pub in Toronto in the 1980's. The wings are $5.95 for eighteen, half price on Tuesday nights. The "six pack" includes wings, chicken fingers, tacos, french fries, nachos, and carrot sticks for $6.75. It's a fairly large place, with upstairs and downstairs rooms, and patio for the summer.

679 Kingston Rd. (near Main St.)
699-9969
Hours: 11 A.M. to 1 A.M. Monday to
 Saturday, Noon to 11 P.M. Sunday

Closed: Christmas Day
Licensed: Full
Payment: Visa, MasterCard, AmEx
Parking: Parking lots at side and rear

FEATHER'S

 The food is genuine English pub and so is much of the atmosphere. Steak-and-kidney pie is $6.50 for dinner; fish and chips are $4.50 and are only served at lunch. The Regency chicken seems to be inspired by medieval meals — it's a boneless breast cooked in honey and wine and served with apples and green pepper ($6.50). And, of course, there's roast beef and Yorkshire pudding ($7.95). The flavor of the food is hearty and it tastes homemade.

Feather's has a tremendous range of draft beers, and claims to be the first place in Toronto that served real ale.

962 Kingston Rd.

694-0443

Hours: 11:30 A.M. to 1 A.M. Monday to Saturday, Noon to 11 P.M. Sunday

Closed: Never

Licensed: Full

Payment: Visa, MasterCard, AmEx

Parking: Some on street and side streets

YONGE AND ST. CLAIR

This isn't a gastronomic area so much as a geographical designation. North of St. Clair Avenue, near Delisle Court, Bregman's has excellent bagels (especially the pumpernickel), and sweet, nutty chelsea buns for takeout. South of St. Clair the string of food shops between Summerhill Avenue and Roxborough Street has wonderful food, although the prices are daunting. Stop in at All The Best Breads for whole wheat bread and at Patachou for a croissant. The croissants and the Basque cake at Le Petit Gourmet shouldn't be missed. Saturday morning brunching at Le Petit Gourmet is a local ritual.

ROSEDALE DINER

This small and casual café was a greasy spoon for forty years, until its reincarnation a few years ago. There are still bar stools and tiny tables in the front, but at the back is a cozy room that looks like tearooms did way back when. The food is good and generally low priced, especially for that area. The large menu changes drastically every few weeks, but recommended constants include Tonawanda wings ($4.95 for eleven — the owners claim to have introduced these famous Buffalo wings to Toronto); calamari ($4.95); hummus with pita, and good daily soups and desserts. The owners also operate the By The Way Café and the Southern Accent restaurant.

1164 Yonge St. (near Summerhill Ave.)
923-3122
Hours: Noon to 1 A.M. Monday to
   Friday, 11 A.M. to 1 A.M. Saturday,
   11 A.M. to 11 P.M. Sunday
Takeout also

Closed: Christmas Day
Licensed: Full
Payment: Visa, MasterCard, AmEx
Parking: Parking across the street

CROW'S NEST PIZZA & OTHER FINE FOODS

Pizza is the dish to order here, with a choice of a thin or thick crust, and whole wheat or regular flour. Choice of toppings varies the price from $4.50 to $6.50. The chicken fingers are the second most popular dish, but they're a far second ($5.95). The Crow's Nest is packed at lunch time.

55 St. Clair Ave. W.
921-0860
Hours: Noon to midnight Monday to
    Saturday, 4 P.M. to 10 P.M. Sunday

Closed: Major Jewish holidays,
    Christmas Day
Licensed: Full
Payment: Visa, MasterCard
Parking: Some on street; parking lot on
    Rosehill Ave.

RHODES

Rhodes is beautifully decorated in uptown-chic, with marble floors, light oak, and lots of plants. You can have almost anything you want here, from steak to fresh fish, to whomping great desserts. It is included here because if you bypass the fancy food, you can also have one of the best hamburgers in town, with french fries as good as those at L'Entrecote, for $5.95. The hamburger is huge, like those at the Senator and at Fuddruckers, very juicy, and cooked over charcoal. I asked for it rare and it came rare. Plain with frites, the hamburger is $5.25. With bacon, cheese, red pepper, and lettuce, it's $5.95. The Caesar salad ($4.50) also is very good, and if you should be inclined to spend some money on dessert, the profiteroles with ice cream on raspberry puree, with chocolate sauce on top, will make you very happy for $3.25.

1496 Yonge St. (north of St. Clair Ave. W.)
968-9315
Hours: 11:30 A.M. to 11:30 P.M. Monday to Friday, 11 A.M. to 11 P.M. Saturday, 11 A.M. to 10:30 P.M. Sunday

Closed: Christmas Day
Licensed: Full
Payment: Visa, MasterCard, AmEx
Parking: Parking lot behind Delisle Court

SCARAMOUCHE PASTA BAR

Down a few steps from the elevated and spiffy Scaramouche Restaurant is a pasta bar, where you can have a wonderful pasta meal at a reasonable cost. The bar is luxurious, yet comfy. Green fettuccine with pancetta and shiitake mushrooms is $8.50; seafood linguine is $10.50. A large selection of wines may be bought by the glass.

1 Benvenuto Place (at Avenue Rd.,
   south of St. Clair Ave. W.)
961-8011
Hours: 6 P.M. to midnight Monday to
   Saturday

Closed: Statutory holidays
Licensed: Full
Payment: Visa, MasterCard, AmEx
Parking: Free valet parking

YONGE AND EGLINTON / MOUNT PLEASANT

This area has grown so quickly, it's easy to lose count of the number of new places — especially hamburger eateries — that keep springing up to service the high schools, and high-rise businesses and residences. There are a great many pubs and some of them have good food, but the emphasis is on business camaraderie during the day and the frolicking single life at night. Try Oliver's, on Yonge Street a few blocks north of Eglinton Avenue, for takeout, especially croissants, breads, and pasta.

YITZ'S DELICATESSEN

This casual, brightly colored eatery has been satisfying people's cravings for smoked meat for nearly fifteen years. The pastrami sandwich is huge, with wheels of rye bread and a generous amount of meat. The corned beef sandwich is just as good, with five ounces of meat for $4.25. Both sandwiches include cole slaw. There's chicken soup with matzo balls for $2.25, and a wonderful soup-meal of boiled beef in clear broth with matzo balls and carrots, served with potato latkes (pancakes) for $8.25. Sandwiches and other specialties are available for takeout, of course. Note the impressive collection of imported cigars.

346 Eglinton Ave. W. (corner of Avenue Rd.)
487-4506
Hours: 10 A.M. to 9 P.M. seven days
Takeout also

Closed: Major Jewish holidays, Christmas Day, New Year's Day
Licensed: Full
Payment: Visa, MasterCard, AmEx
Parking: Street; side streets

LICK'S BURGER & ICE CREAM

 The opening of this latest branch of Lick's means that there is a large burger place on every block around the Yonge Street and Eglinton Avenue intersection. That means some heavy competition, but Lick's was loved already for its fat burgers and plentiful toppings ($2.35). Its first location in the Beach area (see listing in The Beach) became so famous that it paved the way for the opening of this one. There are those who say the burgers taste different here — not as good — but I have been unable to detect any difference. Maybe burgers just taste better in The Beach.

2245 Yonge Street (corner of Eglinton
    Ave. E.)
440-0523
Hours: 11 A.M. to 11 P.M. seven days

Closed: Christmas Day
Licensed: No
Payment: Cash only
Parking: Some on street, side streets

BURGER ON TAP

The name comes from the fact that the burgers are called beerburgers* because they're made with beer (described on the menu as one of Canada's finest lagers which, at the time of research, was Labatt's Blue). We might have known that someone else would figure out a way to eat beer. Some of us have been eating it for years in Welsh rarebit, which is also on the menu here. But don't come for the Welsh rarebit sauce, nor for the atmosphere, which is aggressively bright with shiny red and yellow plastic.

Come just for the fries, which are the best in the neighborhood — even better than Lick's.

Come too for the burgers, 4½ ounces of meat marinated in beer. They are cooked right through, more than I like, and topped with any of a long list of vegetables and condiments that the waitress will recite for you. This is the only burger place I've found so far that routinely serves the burger on a whole wheat roll.

Prices are low, especially for the area: a plate of fries costs 99 cents; a beerburger is $2.29, and a double burger is $3.49. The combos are good deals: the beerburger combo includes fries and a small drink for $3.39; Le Pak includes a fat burger, fries, a small draft, a beer muffin, and coffee or tea, for $6.66.

An effort has been made to evoke some wholesome nostalgia by the old-fashioned milkshake and the buttermilk biscuits. Both are too sweet. The beerchili* (chunky beef chili) is chunky all right — it has lots of meat — and is a meal for $2.29, but it doesn't have much wham.

This looks like part of a chain, but it isn't — so far. Table service is provided only after 6 P.M. Monday through Saturday and

*Registered trademark of Burger on Tap Inc.

all day Sunday. Otherwise it's counter service like at Harvey's: tell them what you want, then tell them what you want on it. By the time you get to the end of the counter, it's yours.

2360 Yonge St. (just north of Eglinton Ave. W.)
487-2801
Hours: 11 A.M. to 1 A.M. Monday to Thursday, 11 A.M. to 2 A.M. Friday, 11 A.M. to 1 A.M. Saturday, 4 P.M. to 11 P.M. Sunday

Closed: Every major holiday
Licensed: Wine and beer
Payment: Visa
Parking: Some on street; municipal lot nearby

THE RED LANTERN

The biggest surprise about this place, according to the many people who recommend it, is not that it's so good, but that it's there at all. Merton Street is more known for its factories than its food. The Red Lantern is hidden among the industrial buildings, marked only by a small neon sign. Walk downstairs and you come into a room with a fair-sized bar, wooden booths, and tables with red-checkered cloths usually filled with people. A stage in the center is used for live entertainment seven nights a week. The atmosphere and service are very friendly.

Pizza is the best thing to order ($4.75 for a medium plain, 60 cents per extra topping). Reminiscent of a deep dish pizza, it comes with a generous topping of cheese and a good flaky crust. The fresh mushroom pizza is especially good. Burgers also are generous in size and tasty ($2.25 to $3.15). Chicken wings are Buffalo-style, eight for $2.75, or 15 cents each on Mondays. Ball players like to come on Monday nights for the foot-long hot dogs at $2.50.

288 Merton St. (west off Mount Pleasant Ave., two blocks south of Davisville Ave.)

483-9444

Hours: 11:30 A.M. to 1 A.M. Monday to Saturday, Noon to 11 P.M. Sunday

Closed: Christmas Eve and Day, New Year's Eve and Day

Licensed: Full

Payment: Visa, MasterCard, AmEx

Parking: Street; parking lots across street and in rear

AFTER ALL

The burgers — all twelve kinds — are very good here. The meat is a juicy and generous serving, the bun nicely offered, and the toppings, which include guacamole, blue cheese, and hot peppercorn, are legion. The club sandwich also is exceptional, served with salad and fries for $6.45. There are daily specials, American beer, and some chic pizzas with pesto, lobster, and such. There also are lots of desserts, some nice salads, and too much noisy music. Note the late closing on weekend nights.

535 Mount Pleasant Rd. (north of
  Davisville Ave.)
488-2000
Hours: 11:30 A.M. to 1 A.M. Monday to
  Thursday, 11:30 A.M. to 2 A.M.
  Friday, Saturday, 11:30 A.M. to 11
  P.M. Sunday
Takeout and delivery also

Closed: Christmas Day, Canada Day
  weekend
Licensed: Full
Payment: Visa, MasterCard, AmEx
Parking: Street

PENROSE FISH & CHIPS

The Penrose has had the reputation of serving some of the best fish and chips in the city for a longer time than any of the competition. It is a small family-run place that was started by the father after the war. The family serves large, wonderful chunks of fresh halibut with very good chips ($2.85 for takeout — wrapped in newspaper; $3.00 to eat it there).

600 Mount Pleasant Rd. (just south of Manor Rd.)
483-6800
Hours: 11 A.M. to 7 P.M. Tuesday to Friday, 11 A.M. to 6:30 P.M. Saturday
Takeout also

Closed: Sunday, Monday; all statutory holidays
Licensed: No
Payment: Cash only
Parking: Street

MOUNT PLEASANT LUNCH

This sixteen-year-old pleasant landmark has always specialized in serving complete dinners for fair prices. Lasagna, made with three cheeses and meat sauce, is served hot in a skillet with garlic bread, soup of the day, and a small Caesar salad for $5.95; veal Parmigiana is as hearty for $8.25. Watch for off-menu specialties like roast rack of pork, pheasant, or quail. The chef, Nick Musella, is also the owner (always a good sign) and takes good care of his special customers.

604 Mount Pleasant Rd. (south of
  Manor Rd.)
481-9331
Hours: 11 A.M. to 11 P.M. Monday to
  Friday, 5 P.M. to 11 P.M. Saturday,
  Sunday

Closed: Christmas Day
Licensed: Full
Payment: Cash, Visa
Parking: Street

CHICK 'N' DELI

A huge plastic chicken on the neon sign marks the location of this bar/restaurant. The door handles are carved chickens and rubber birds hang from the rafters the way that ferns hang in restaurants closer to Yorkville. This is where to go if you like crowds, jazz, and chicken wings, because you're guaranteed to find the steamiest of all three at any time.

The specialty of the house is chicken wings, Buffalo-style, which means crispy and spicy-hot. They come with celery, carrots, and a blue cheese dip, much like they're served at the Anchor Bar in Buffalo and at the Madison Avenue Restaurant in Toronto. One is never sure whether the dip is for the wings or the vegetables, but never mind — you're among friends here. The nachos also are good, big and covered with a zippy meat sauce, then coated in two types of cheese. Olives and pepper slices lend color and bulk to the plate which, like the wings, can serve as a meal, with a couple of drafts to wash it down. I've had good success with the barbecued chicken, but the chicken sandwich was dry and bony.

Sometimes it's hard to pay attention to what you're eating because of the noise of people and the music. There is seating for about 100, but seating is a luxury anytime after 9 A.M. Be prepared to wait.

One of the best times to be here is for Sunday brunch, where for $5.95 you can eat enough eggs, waffles, and wings to do you all day. The best drink is orange juice and champagne at $6.00 a pitcher. Sunday brunch is served from 11 A.M. to 3 P.M..

744 Mount Pleasant Rd. (south of Eglinton Ave. E.)

Hours: 11 A.M. to 1 A.M. Monday to Saturday, 11:30 A.M. to 11 P.M. Sunday

Closed: Christmas Day, New Year's Day

Licensed: Full

Payment: Visa, MasterCard, AmEx

Parking: Small parking lot in front, but it's always full. Check side streets.

EGLINTON AND BATHURST

The three-block strip of Eglinton Avenue from Bathurst Street west to the Allen Expressway is packed with food stores and restaurants. The flavor is Jewish – both European and middle-eastern, although there are some exceptions. In Nortown Plaza, Patachou Patisserie and Café has the best almond croissants in town. Have them for breakfast with a bowl of café au lait so large you have to hold it with two hands.

Take a Sunday to shop the street, stopping at Nortown Meats for the barbecued chicken; at Goldy's for the herring in sour cream and the egg salad; at Daiter's for Gryfe's bagels and their own yogurt; and at Health Bread Bakery across the street for the rye bread, extra heavy with caraway seeds, and the poppy seed bagels.

BAGEL PARADISE LTD.

This is a small, casual eatery that serves generous portions of inexpensive food. Breakfast includes two eggs, bacon, a bagel, and coffee, for $2.65; a big bowl of matzo ball soup is $1.95; bagels and cream cheese cost $2.25 without lox and $5.50 with. Anything with bagels is good and some things are paradise, like the tuna and chopped egg. Everything comes with a bagel. Eat those and skip the pies.

953 Eglinton Ave. W. (west of Bathurst St.)

787-8670

Hours: 7 A.M. to 6 P.M. seven days

Closed: Major Jewish holidays

Licensed: No

Payment: Cash only

Parking: Some on street; paid lots on Eglinton Ave.

JERUSALEM DELICATESSEN

There are two restaurants named "Jerusalem" within one block. One is a full-blown restaurant which, judging by the crowds, needs no further recommendation. The other, the deli, is smaller, more casual, and superb.

Its middle-eastern menu deserves careful reading. Some of the dishes may be unfamiliar, but try them all. The first time, have the Jerusalem burger, as remote from an ordinary burger as Jerusalem is from Orillia. This is a ground lamb patty, heavily spiced and herbed, then laid in a whole pita with some lettuce, and hot sauce drizzled into it. One bite from the top and the bottom begins to leak into your hands, but this is not a place where manners come first. Don't miss the hummus with pine nuts and meat, or the baba ganoush, smoky and smooth, both served with pita. (The way to eat pita is to tear off a triangle, wrap it into a cone, and scoop the mixture into the top.) Other hot pita sandwiches include the shish kebab, filled with more chunks of lamb than you need. Then there are the fried tomatoes, sautéed in olive oil, then liberally soaked in a spicy tomato sauce. The hotter you can convince the cook to make the sauce the better.

967 Eglinton Ave. W.
789-3843
Hours: 11 A.M. to 10 P.M. seven days

Closed: Christmas Day, New Year's Day
Licensed: No
Payment: Cash only
Parking: Street, side streets

BAGEL KING

This is a dairy restaurant with a long counter near the front where all types of bagels and pastries are sold. The bagels and bread are fine, but the pastries are mostly oversweet.

At the tables, order the Dagwood Sandwich for $5.95. It's made by dividing one of the huge twister bagels into three sections and filling each section with a gigantic spread of cream cheese with some lox, egg salad, a piece of lettuce, and salmon salad. It's a very big sandwich, served with a large dollop of cole slaw.

The buttermilk pancakes are terrific, as are the egg dishes, especially the one of scrambled eggs with fried onions and lox. Soups, too, are very good, especially the cabbage borscht or any of the daily specials, including the mushroom or the vegetable. One of the most popular dishes is the Greek salad. This Jewish version features lots of iceberg lettuce, some feta cheese, a few olives, and a hardboiled egg. It's served with a bagel and makes an offbeat lunch for $4.95.

Note the children's menu, which offers peanut butter sandwiches, pancakes, and grilled cheese sandwiches for low prices. The kids are provided with placemats and crayons that may keep them from running to the front counter and pleading for jelly doughnuts or gingerbread men.

1000 Eglinton Ave. W. (west of Bathurst St.)

781-9181

Hours: 7 A.M. to midnight Monday to Friday, 7 A.M. to 1 A.M. Saturday, 8 A.M. to noon Sunday

Closed: Major Jewish holidays

Licensed: No

Payment: Visa, MasterCard

Parking: Street and side street; parking lot on Hilltop Rd.

NORTH OF EGLINTON

This is a very wide area that includes a few far-flung places that are worth the drive. Serious searchers might walk the blocks on Avenue Road north from Eglinton Avenue to Lawrence Avenue. Here there are a lot of established food shops that have serviced the Lawrence Park area for years. On Yonge Street, a half-dozen blocks north of Eglinton Avenue, Pastissima offers a wide variety of takeout pastas and a terrific spicy Italian sausage. A worthy rival is Sanelli's on Yonge Street, north of Lawrence Avenue, for pasta and wonderful accompanying sauces. Cowieson's Meats has single servings of shepherd's pie, and beef and chicken pot pies for reasonable prices.

COMMISSO BROS. & RACCO ITALIAN BAKERY

The hot veal sandwich is made with a huge veal cutlet, homemade tomato sauce, and mozzarella cheese, spiked as fiery as you want with peppers ($2.95). There are also sausage sandwiches and lasagna. All this at any hour of the day or night, because both of Commisso's locations are open twenty-four hours a day.

8 Kincort St. (west of Caledonia Rd., north off Castlefield Ave.)
651-7671
– and –
33 Eddystone Ave. (west off Jane St., south of Finch Ave. W.)
743-6600
Hours: 24 hours, 7 days
Takeout, or eat there standing up

Closed: Never
Licensed: Not at Eddystone; full license at Kincort
Payment: Cash only at Eddystone location; Visa, MasterCard, AmEx at Kincort
Parking: Large parking lots in front of both locations

JACK KWINTER FOODS *(Kwinter's)*

Excellent smoked foods are made right here, and you can smell them as soon as you come in. There are a few stools to perch on while having what most people consider to be Toronto's best hot dog. There are four kinds of hot dogs, which vary according to the beef mixtures and casings used, but none contain suspect fillers and none have more than one percent salt. All hot dogs are served on egg-loaf buns and cost between $1.90 and $2.25. Regulars also go for the smoked roast beef, pastrami or corned beef. The smoked turkey breast is lean and lovely. Take extra home.

780 Steeprock Dr. (west off Dufferin
   St., south of Finch Ave. W. — near
   Idomo)
630-0064
Hours: 8 A.M. to 5 P.M. Monday to
   Friday, 10 A.M. to 2 P.M. Sunday
Takeout also

Closed: Saturday; all statutory holidays
Licensed: No
Payment: Visa
Parking: Parking lot in front

CAMARRA'S PIZZERIA & RESTAURANT

Camarra's is thought by many, including me, to have the best pizza in town. The dough is very bready, thick but light, and all the toppings are fresh. Mrs. Valentini, the owner, says that the dough stays soft, even for leftovers the next day, but I've never had a leftover Camarra's pizza to confirm this. Also good is the calzone, which is dough stuffed with ham, capicollo, and Emmenthal cheese, shaped into a half-moon and baked ($4.00). The pasta dishes, like lasagna are okay, but you come here for the pizza. At $8.10 in the dining room and $7.15 takeout for a thirteen-inch pizza, it's pricier than most.

2899 Dufferin St. (south of Lawrence Ave. W.)

789-3221

Hours: 11:30 A.M. to 11 P.M. Monday, Wednesday, Thursday, 11:30 to 1 A.M. Friday, Saturday, 4 P.M. to 11 P.M. Sunday

Takeout and delivery also

Closed: Tuesday; Christmas Day, New Year's Day, Easter, Thanksgiving

Licensed: Full

Payment: Visa, MasterCard, AmEx

Parking: Parking in front

KATZ'S DELI &
CORNED BEEF EMPORIUM

The pastrami and corned beef sandwiches ($3.75) are the specialty here, should you find yourself hungry near the Yorkdale shopping center. On Friday or Saturday, have a bowl of split pea, barley and mushroom, or chicken soup with matzo balls.

3222 Dufferin Ave. (north of Lawrence Ave. W.)
782-1111
Hours: 8:30 A.M. to 10 P.M. Monday to Friday, 8:30 A.M. to 8:30 P.M. Saturday

Closed: Sunday; all major holidays
Payment: MasterCard, AmEx, Diners Club
Parking: Large parking lot

BAGEL WORLD COFFEE SHOP

The superb, fresh bagels will probably be what first brings you here and then brings you back, despite the astounding lineups on Sundays. Then you'll notice a lot of happy people eating lots of other things. At lunch, nearly everyone has soup or blintzes with lots of sour cream. The egg dishes are very popular here, as they are in most of the dairy restaurants. Prices are terrific: a lunch of eggs and onions with a twister bagel (wonderful twisters!) is $2.65. Potato latkes are 75 cents plain or 90 cents with sour cream or applesauce. The refined should note that all the dishes are paper throwaway, and that the atmosphere is very casual — customers share tables whether they know each other or not; impatient diners rise to serve themselves coffee and bagels; and waitresses call across the room to one another and to customers. It's a lot like home, but the food is better.

---

336 Wilson Ave. W. (west of Bathurst St.)
635-5931
Hours: 5 A.M. to 10 P.M. Sunday to Friday, 5 A.M. to 11 P.M. Saturdays

Closed: Major Jewish holidays
Licensed: No
Payment: Cash
Parking: Some parking in front of restaurant

UNITED BAKERS
DAIRY RESTAURANT

This big new branch of the long-loved 338 Spadina Avenue restaurant has gone Hollywood with great success, featuring skylights, and lots of tables. Tables are scarce at even the oddest hours, because the food is wonderful. It's a dairy restaurant, which means that nothing with meat is ever offered — but that doesn't mean you can't get good and full. Always order the soups ($1.75), which are rich and fulsome — particularly the mushroom and barley soup, the pea soup (which contains noodles), or the beet borscht. The gefilte fish (a large patty made with ground pike and simmered in fish broth) is the best in the city. It's served with a very hot homemade beet horseradish which, when used in small amounts, is a perfect foil for the subtle flavor of the fish. The blintzes (like cheese crepes) also are the best than can be found. Huge and generously filled, they are served with applesauce and sour cream ($5.25). An order of Mr. Brown's French toast is two very thick slices of bread, soaked in egg, then deep fried. It's a caloric bomb that will take you back to childhood. There's a large menu, with each specialty well worth trying. Breakfast specials Monday to Friday cost $1.49 and $2.49.

Lawrence Plaza (northwest corner of
Bathurst St. and Lawrence Ave. W.)
789-0519
Hours: 7 A.M. to 10 P.M. Monday to
Thursday, 7 A.M. to 8 P.M. Friday, 7
A.M. to midnight Saturday, (Summer
hours: 7 A.M. to 9 P.M.), 9 A.M. to 9
P.M. Sunday

Closed: Major Jewish holidays
Licensed: No
Payment: Visa, MasterCard
Parking: Ample parking in plaza

BLACK CAT FISH & CHIPS

The fish is halibut only, and its batter is thin and crisper than most. Chips are homemade, usually from Prince Edward Island potatoes. An order of fish and chips is $3,40, including tax. The fried scallops also are good ($6.00 with chips). There are a few tables in this very casual place, or you can take your order out. Gus Karahalios, who has owned Black Cat for eighteen years, plans to enlarge the premises.

1929 Avenue Rd. (south of Wilson Ave. W.)
789-1555
Hours: 8 A.M. to 8 P.M. Monday to Saturday
Takeout also

Closed: Sunday; statutory holidays except Good Friday
Licensed: No
Payment: Cash only
Parking: Street; municipal lot nearby

POOR WILLIAM'S FINE FOOD
RESTAURANT & TAKE OUT

Paul Carpenco, who trained at the Windsor Arms, and his brother, John, dreamed of running a small neighborhood restaurant that served good home-cooked food at reasonable prices. They gave Poor William a home, and if what he needed was good, warming soups and terrific desserts, he got it in this warmly appointed restaurant. Soups of the day may include broccoli and cheddar cheese, leek and potato, or cabbage borscht. All are served with homemade buttermilk biscuits for $2.25 or $2.95. Desserts too are exceptional, especially the sour cream-strawberry-rhubarb pie. The main courses vary by season and availability and are okay, but aren't in the same league as the soups and desserts.

2721 Yonge St. (north of Blythwood Rd.)

487-3934

Hours: 11:30 A.M. to 11 P.M. Sunday to Wednesday, 11:30 A.M. to midnight Thursday to Saturday

Takeout also (10 percent off)

Closed: Week between Christmas and New Year's

Licensed: Full

Payment: Visa, MasterCard, AmEx

Parking: Street; Parking lot at back

PICKUP'S FISH & CHIPS

 Situated in a one-storey rundown mall, this tiny three-table place has been here for about eight years and has still stayed a secret to all but the locals.

Pickup's fish and chips are superb: the fish is made from big chunks of fresh halibut and the chips are their own (not so the onion rings.) The entire menu is made up of variations on these, plus a tart, lightly dressed coleslaw that shouldn't be missed — especially at $1.00 for a huge pile of it.

If you take your order out, they'll cram your food into boxes that are too small for the great amount they give you, then wrap the whole thing together in newsprint, held together by a rubber band. So, if you do take it out, eat it soon, before the steam makes the crispy batter soft. Note the hours: like most fish and chip shops, Pickup's closes early.

246 Sheppard Ave. W. (near Yonge St.)
Hours: 11 A.M. to 7 P.M. Monday to
    Friday, Noon to 7 P.M. Saturday

Closed: Sunday
Licensed: No
Payment: Cash only
Parking: In front

THE PICKLE BARREL

The extensive menu in this long-loved eatery will provide nearly everything you might think of having in a deli — and then some. Recommended are the deli sandwiches of smoked meat on rye with coleslaw, fries, and pickle slices ($3.95). I also like the Caesar salad and the potato skins.

5941 Leslie St. (near Finch Ave. W. — also in the Atrium on Bay downtown)

493-4944

Hours: 9 A.M. to 1 A.M. seven days

Closed: Christmas Day

Licensed: Full

Payment: Visa, AmEx

Parking: Plaza parking